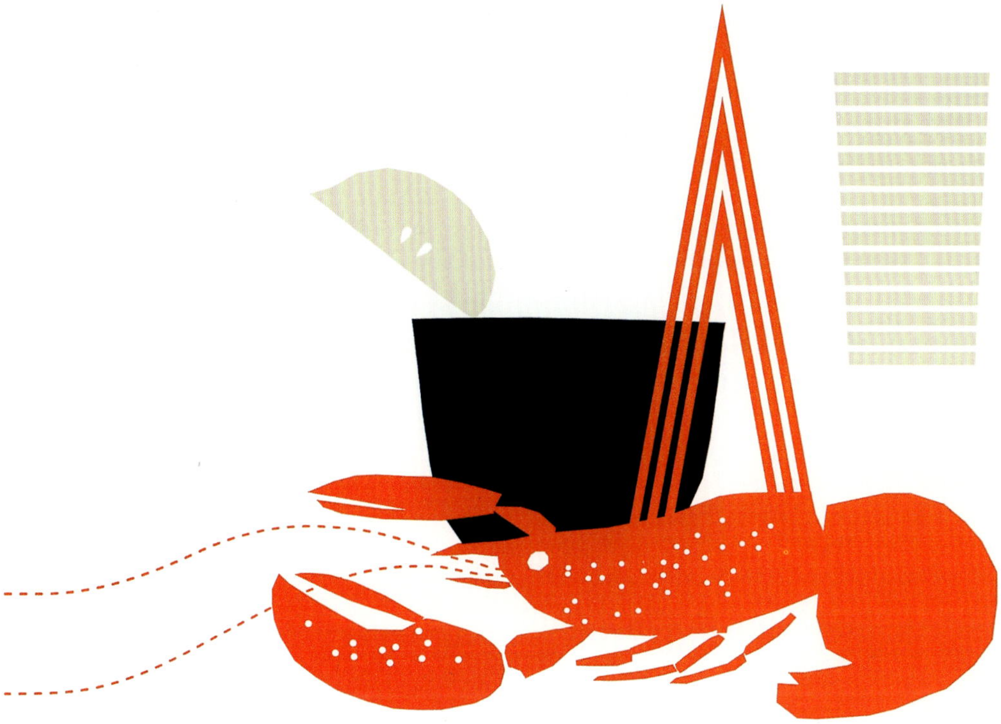

More Autopsy Than Diagnosis

• COMPETITIVENESS REVEALS AN INSECURE CORE ONLY SATIATED BY OTHERS' PRAISE •

• LEFT WITH AN UNCEASING PRESSURE • THE HEAVILY GUARDED PECKING ORDER NEVER ALLOWS REST • THE TIGHTROPE WALK OF CONFIDENCE •

• A FEW VISUAL GIMMICKS MASK CONSERVATIVE, ILL THOUGHT OUT, DESPERATE PLEAS FOR ATTENTION •

All we are and what we're not.

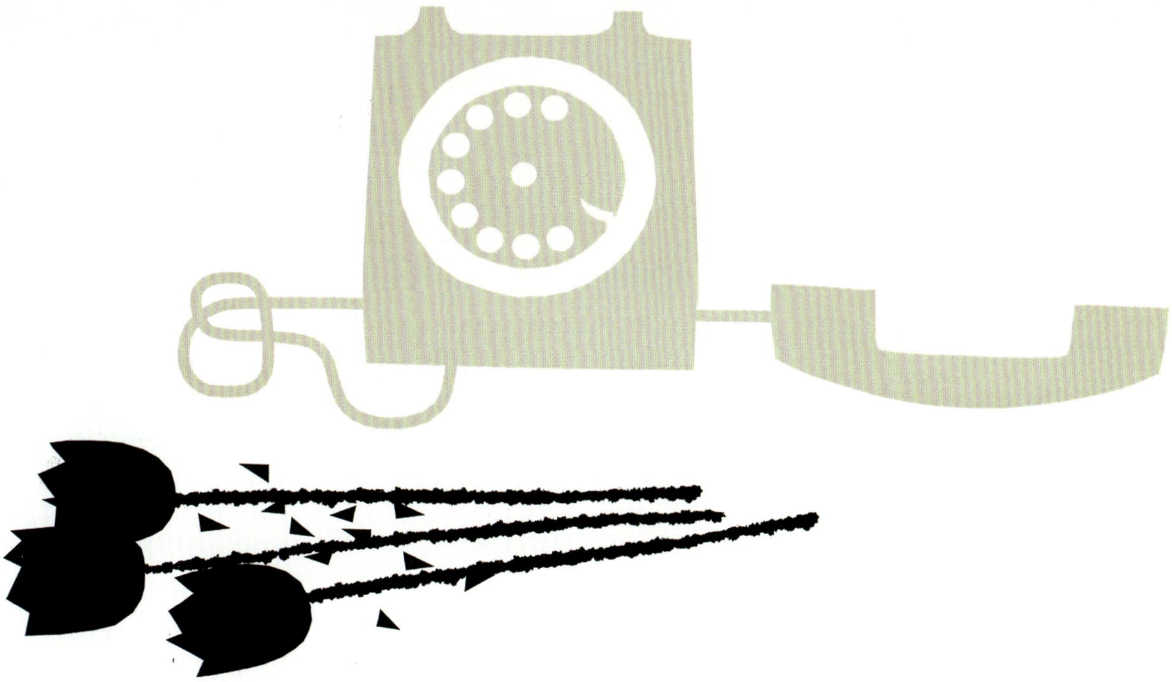

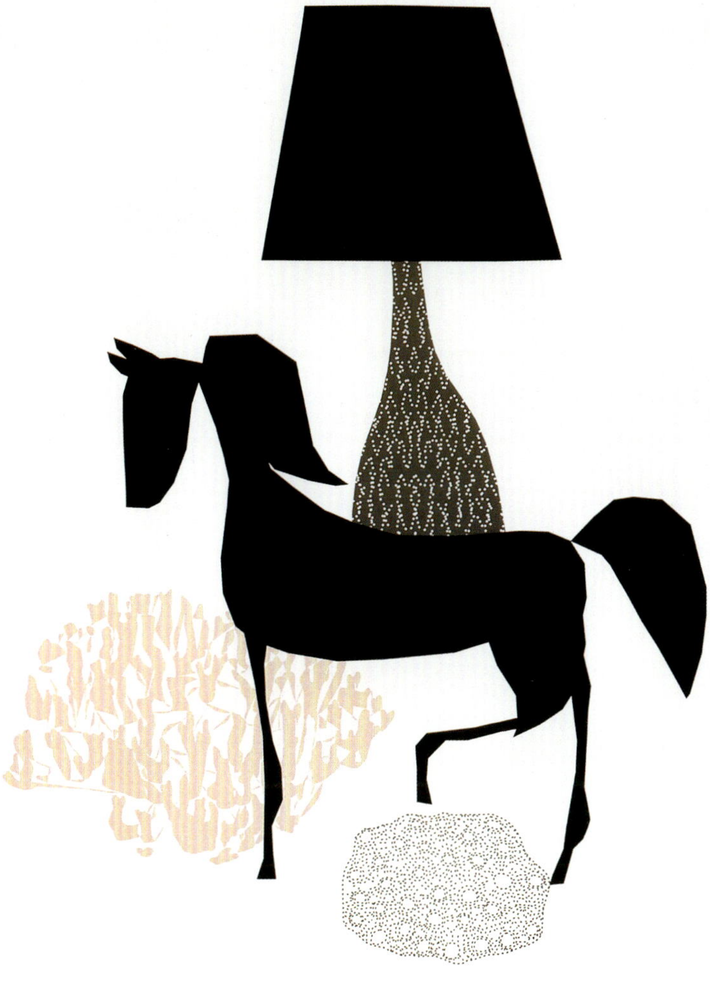

Don’t Call, Don’t Even Write

• IT’S HARD TO SAY • I’M ASSUMING THE ANSWER WAS NO • DIDN’T SAY A WORD • THREW THAT RING IN THE TRASH •
• THE FRIENDS LEFT BEHIND • THE CHEAP SUBSTITUTES FOR TALENT • THE LATE NIGHTS & MISSED MEETINGS • THE COFFEE IN YOUR LAP •
• HOW IT SHOULD HAVE BEEN • HOW IT WAS • I DIDN’T WANT TO BE THE ONE TO TELL YOU •

Just one more minute. I've already called the ambulance. You're going to make it. I know you are. And all those things I said, well I never meant them. You weren't the last person on my mind. And when I said ... I was lying.

We study the wall label. Forming an image of the artist from a last name, birthplace & date of birth. From a title and a list of materials. He's younger than I thought. He's a she. She's actually from Europe. It's more than cardboard. It took him three years to make this. It's owned by what's his name.

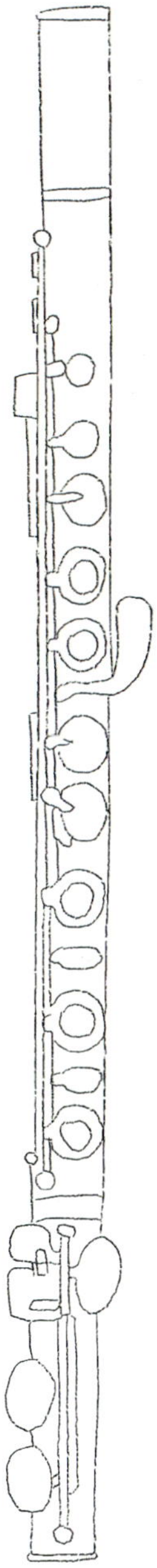

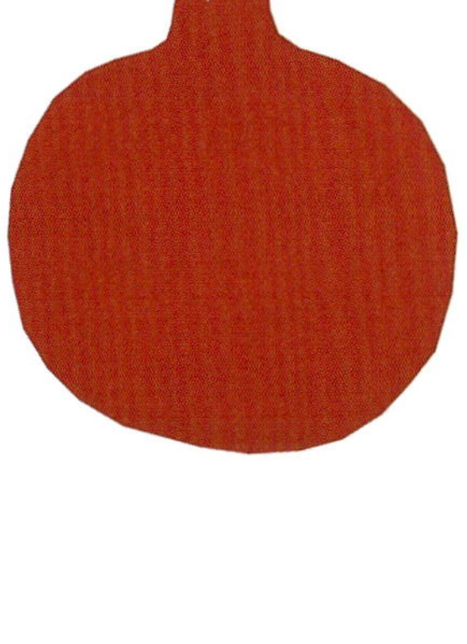

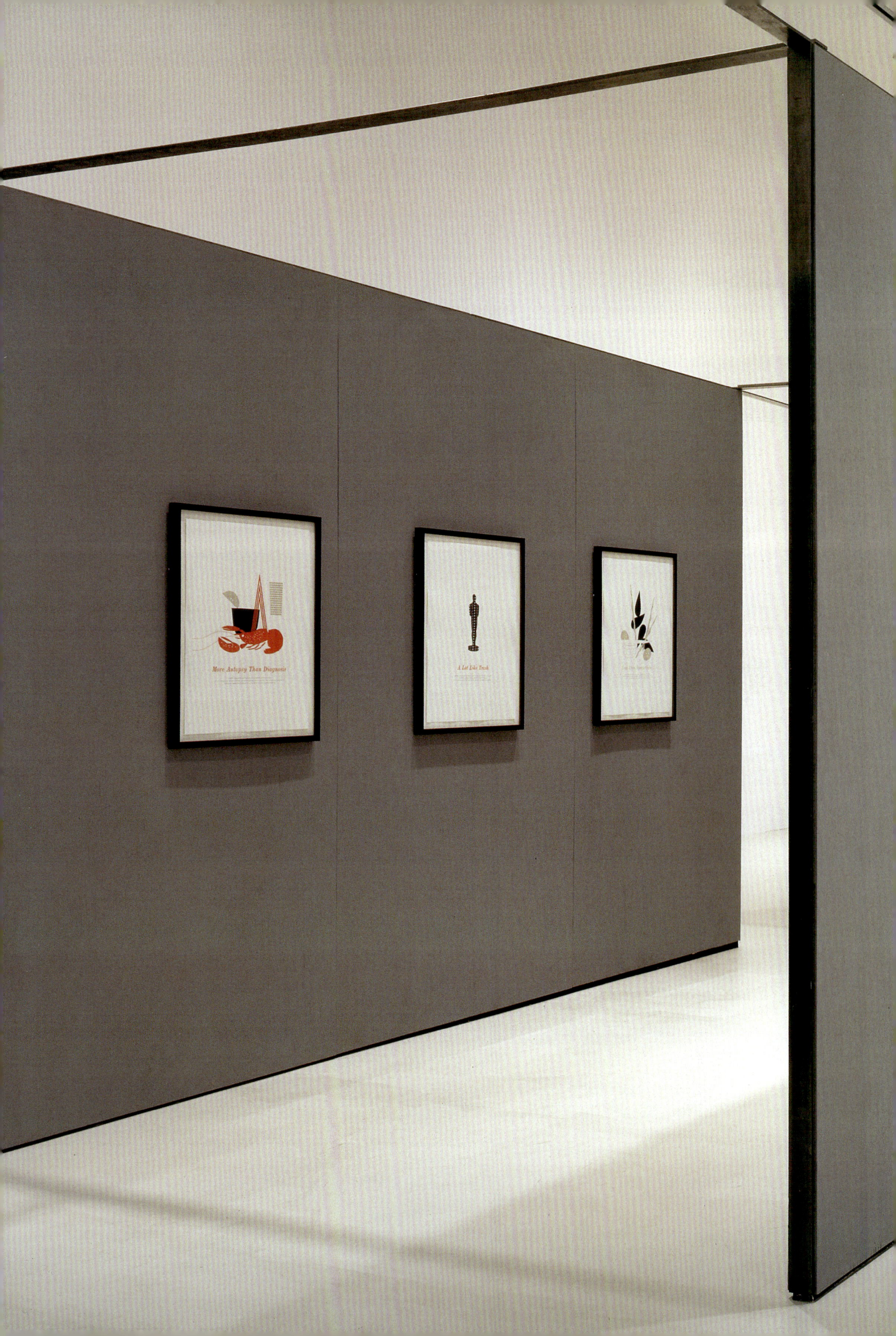
More Autopsy Than Diagnosis
A Lot Like Trash

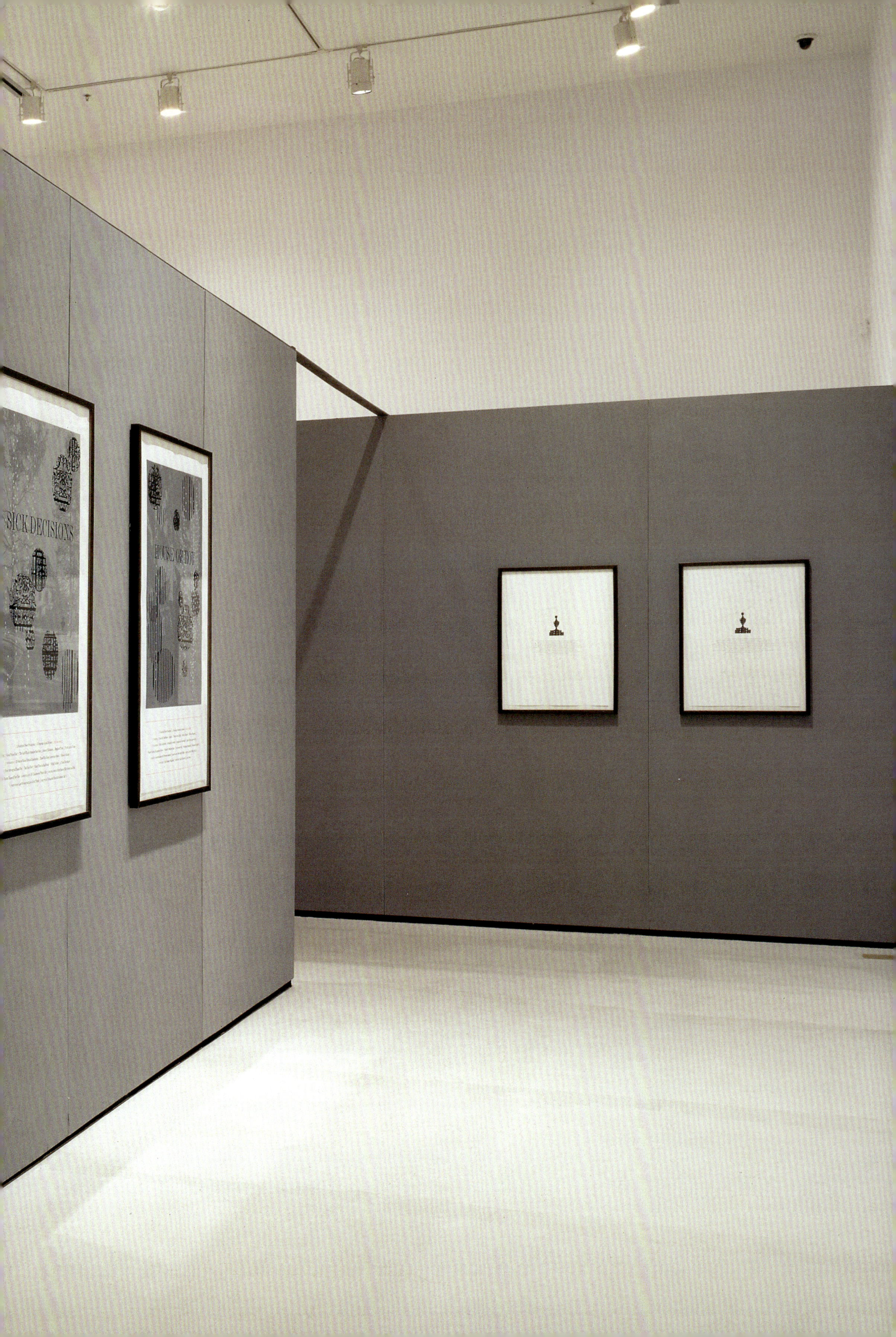
SICK DECISIONS
HOUSE OF ROT

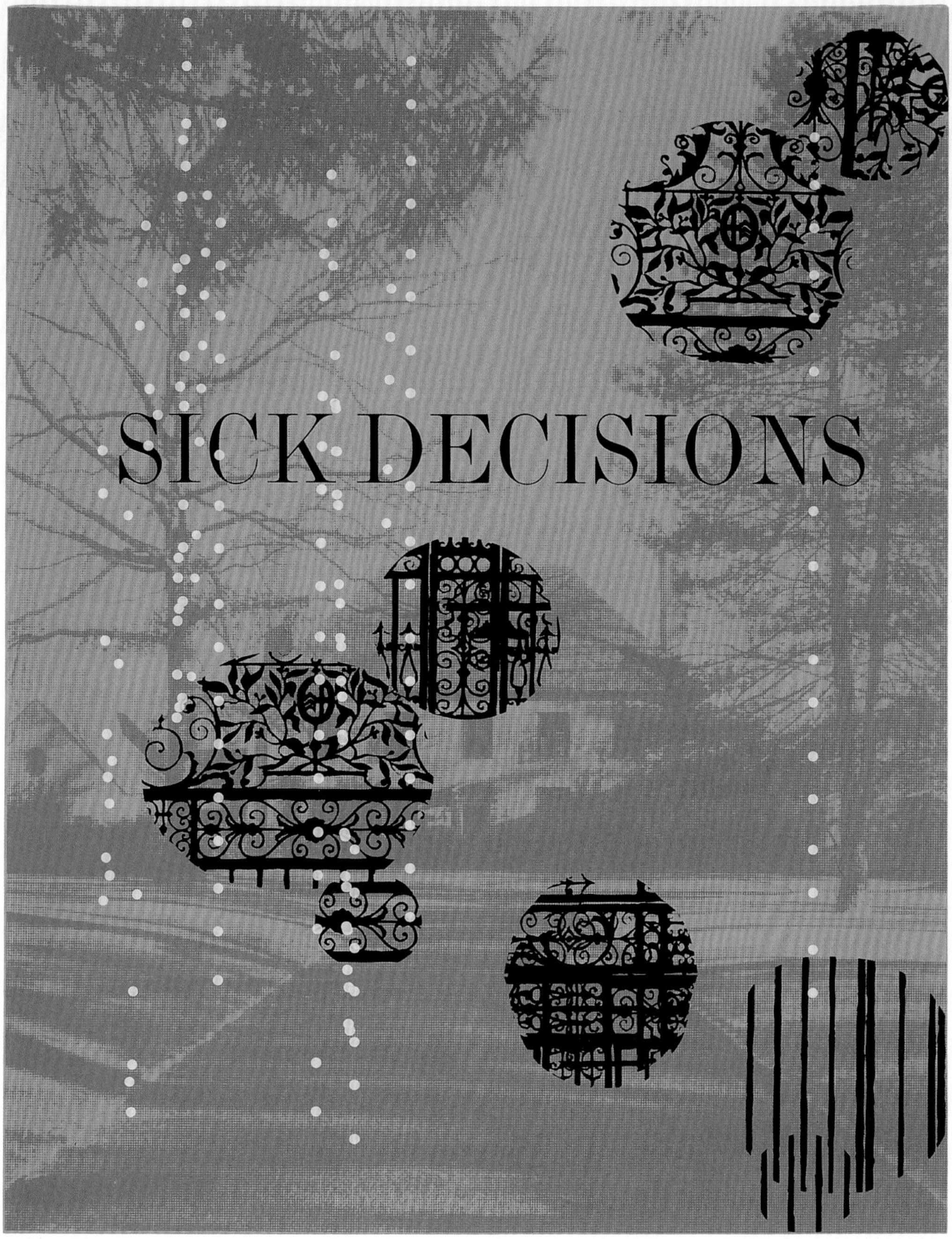

‡ A Frustrated Power Production ‡ A Desperate Appeal Release ‡ Sick Decisions ‡

‡ STARRING ‡ Good Prison Visit ‡ The Guilt Which Organizes Your Fear ‡ Abuse of Education ‡ Misplaced Trust ‡ Not for Lack of Funds ‡

‡ CO-STARRING ‡ 25 Years of Value, Virtue & Leadership ‡ Those Who Enjoy Correcting Others ‡ Videos on Valium ‡

‡ Poor Attempt at Thank You ‡ Past Your Best ‡ Great Titles for Bad Books ‡ Pitiful Portion ‡ A Name You Regret ‡

‡ MUSIC BY Victim Danse & Turn Pale ‡ SCREENPLAY BY 101 Unanswered Phone Calls ‡ ORIGINAL STORY BY Bret Easton Ellis's Head on a Plate ‡

‡ PRODUCED BY Last Attempt at Love & Soft Teeth ‡ DIRECTED BY Exhausted Blood & Imitation Salt ‡

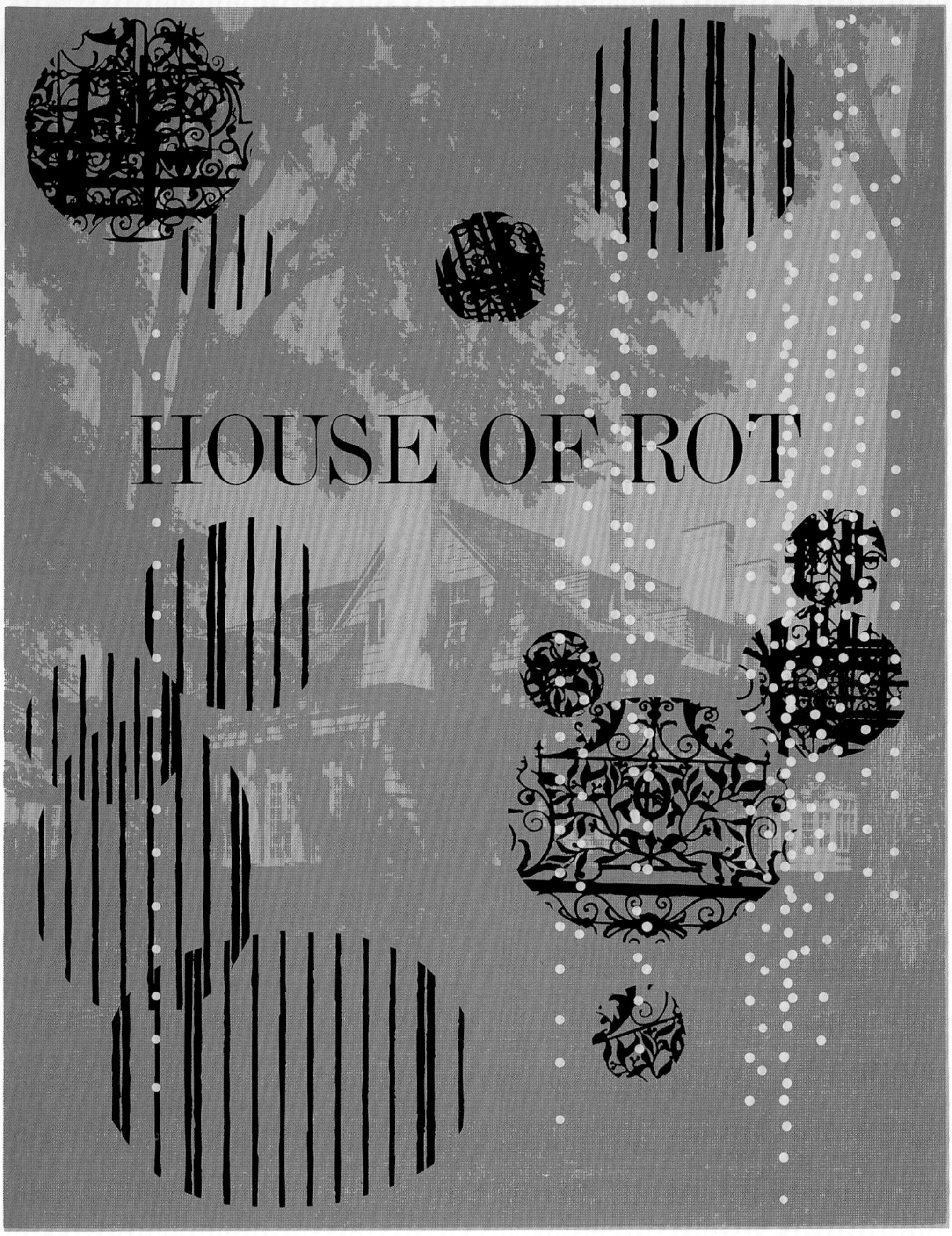

‡ A Frustrated Power Production ‡ A Decadent Medication Release ‡ House of Rot ‡

‡ STARRING ‡ Unchecked Confidence ‡ Assplay ‡ 7 Years in One Night ‡ Parlor of Regret ‡ Divorce Magazine ‡

‡ CO-STARRING ‡ Effort Judgement ‡ Revealing Comment ‡ Complain to Understand ‡ Layers Upon Layers of Fat ‡

‡ Wasted Contact & Expensive Advice ‡ Defined by What You Hate ‡ Psychotropic Gift ‡ Belligerent Euphoria ‡ Knee-jerk Negativity ‡

‡ MUSIC BY Carpeted Quote with Perverse Ambition ‡ SCREENPLAY BY Diet Coke & Vodka ‡ ORIGINAL STORY BY Black Am. Ex. ‡

‡ PRODUCED BY Night Sweats & Slug Bait ‡ DIRECTED BY Love Under Will Under Stress ‡

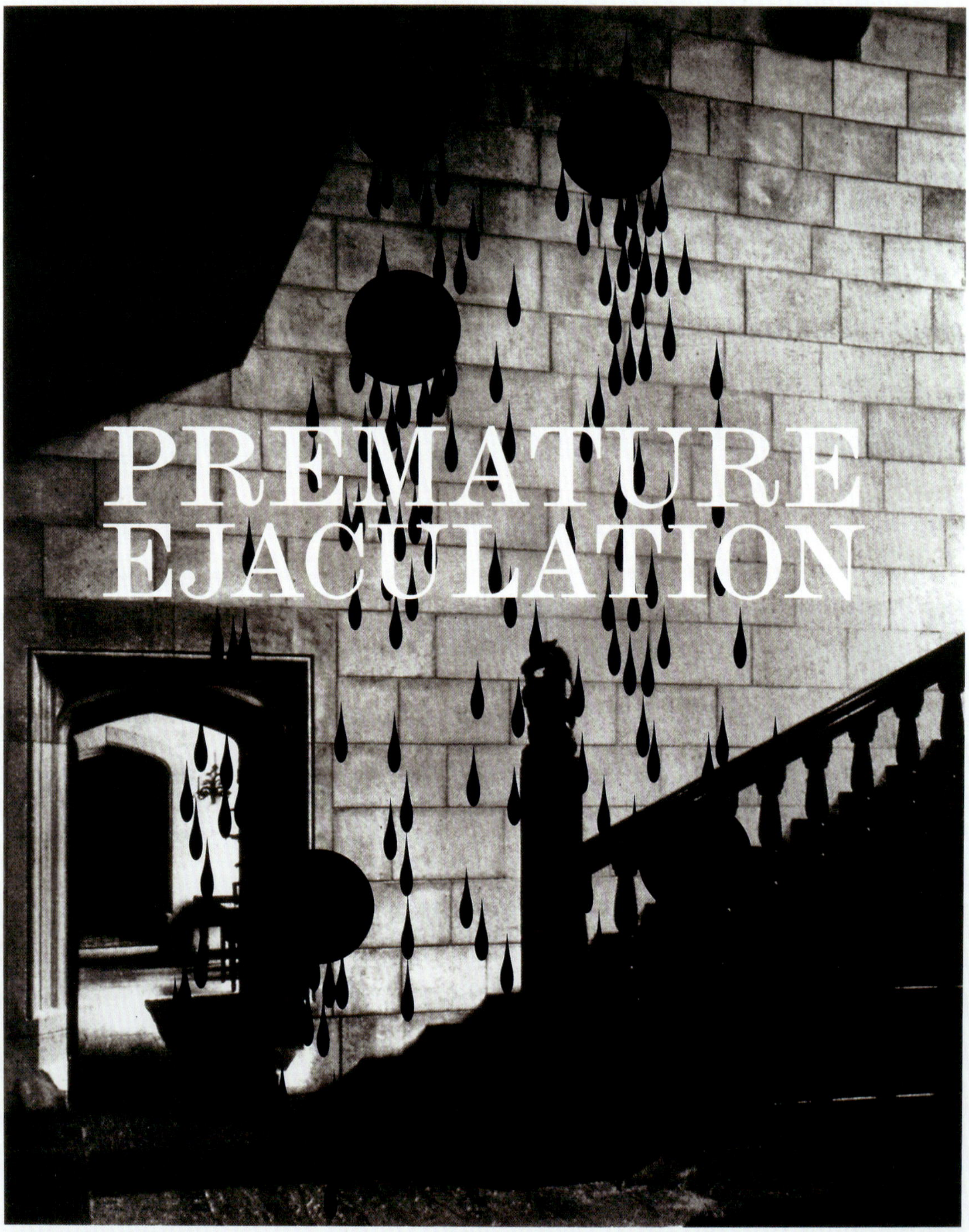

TORN APART PICTURES PRESENTS • A NEVER THAT LASTS FOREVER RELEASE • A HOLLOW NEST FILM • PREMATURE EJACULATION
STARRING • THE DISAPPOINTMENTS OF KENNETH ANGER • THE SMELLS OF DEATH • GRAY WOLVES SIPPING CHIANTI • THE GRUESOME GUESTS • A SADISTIC DJ
CO-STARRING • BRUISED ARMS & WET CIGARETTES • PARTY WITH YOUR PUBERTY • BROKEN GATES • PASS OUT WALLET DUMP • WET STEAMING PANT MEAT
PRODUCED BY • FANS OF FAKES & FANS OF FILTH • CREDIBILITY GAINS - CONFIDENCE LOST • SWOLLEN ACTOR • ORIGINAL MUSIC BY • SEMEN OF SEVEN SICK SERVANTS
WRITTEN BY • RECREATIONAL DRUG ABUSE • BASED ON THE NOVEL • TROPICAL ITCH ICE PICK • DIRECTED BY • SINK FULL OF BLOOD

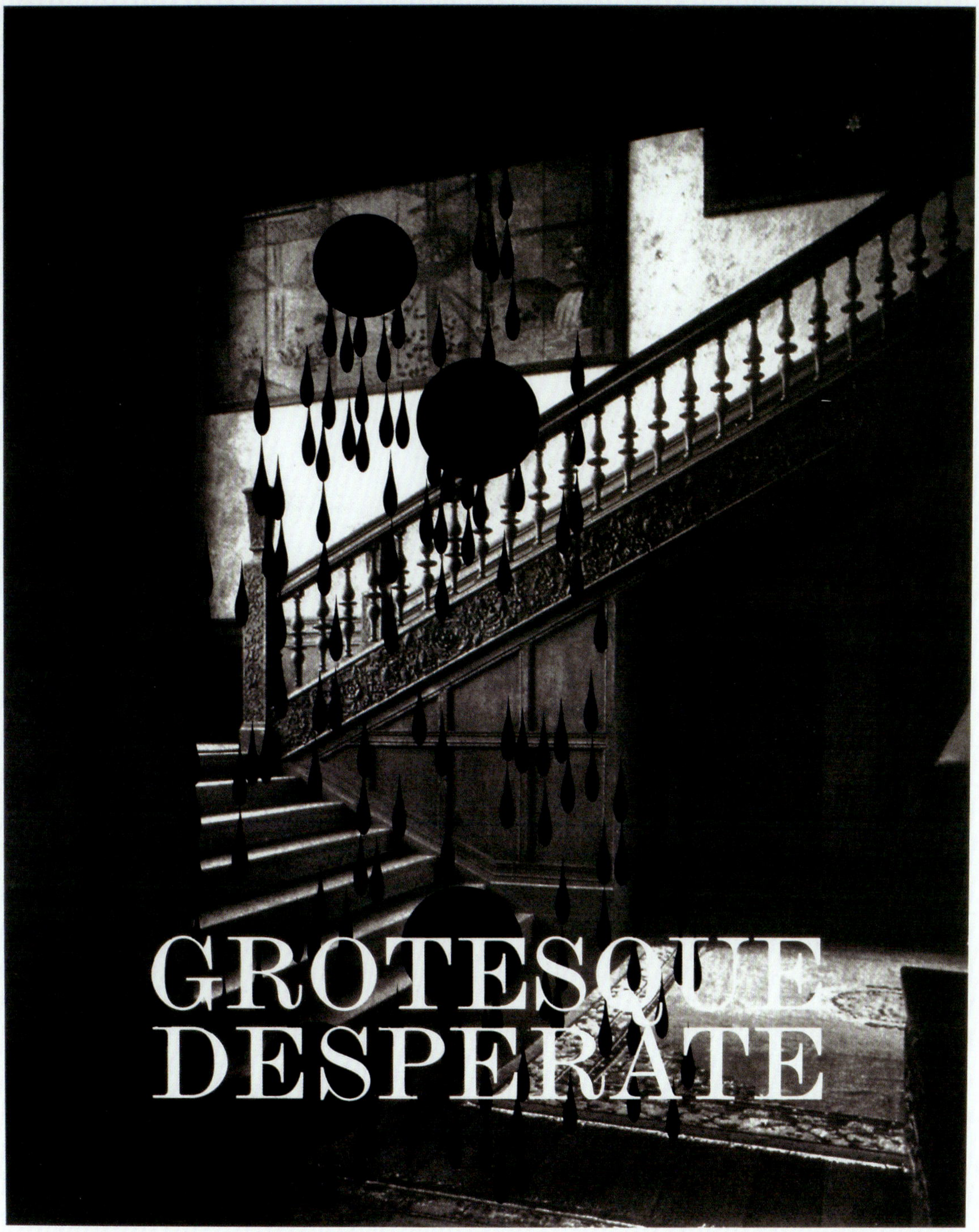

AN INABILITY TO MAKE DECISIONS PRESENTS • AN ATROCIOUS IRRITANT PRODUCTION OF • GROTESQUE DESPERATE
STARRING • POT OF COFFEE AS DEFENSE • TWINS WITHOUT TALENT • DEAD INXS MEMBER • BLAND WELCOME & OBVIOUS MISTRUST • A THANKLESS HANDJOB
DARBY CRASH'S SWEATY COFFIN • PRODUCED BY • HORROR CALLED PUBLIC • MAIMED PRIDE & CHALLENGED SELF-ESTEEM • THE BROWN BUBBLY
MUSIC BY • PROSTITUTES OF THE DEAD & AMATEUR SADO EROTIC DRAWINGS • ALCOHOLIC BONFIRE OF IDEAS • THE APOCALYPSE IS A JOKE
STORY BY • LOS ANGELES STILLBIRTH & THE LEISURE CLASS • DIRECTED BY • WRISTS SLIT WITH BROKEN GLASS IN AN EMPTY BATHTUB IN A FOREIGN COUNTRY

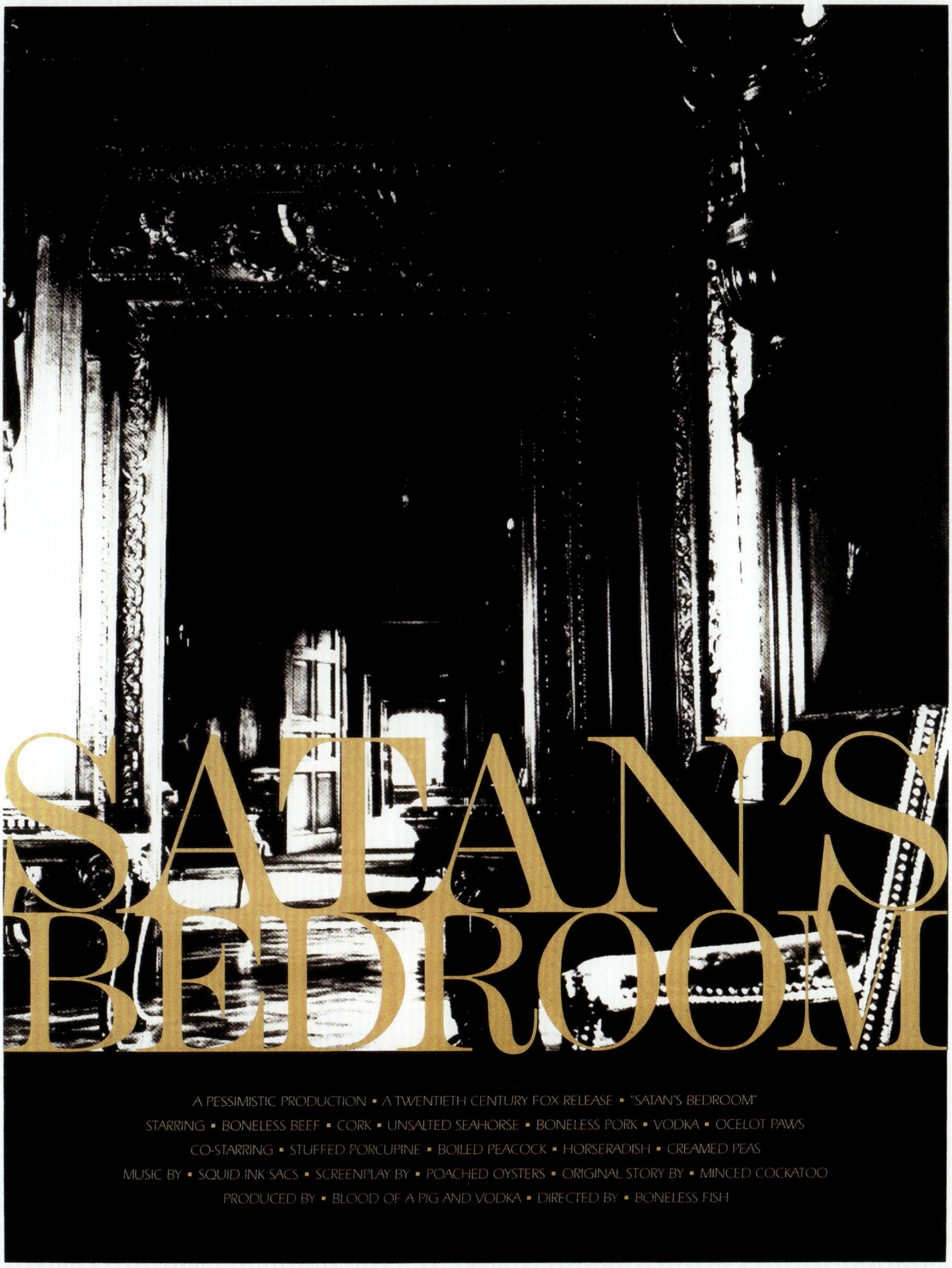
SATAN'S
BEDROOM
A PESSIMISTIC PRODUCTION ▪ A TWENTIETH CENTURY FOX RELEASE ▪ "SATAN'S BEDROOM"
STARRING ▪ BONELESS BEEF ▪ CORK ▪ UNSALTED SEAHORSE ▪ BONELESS PORK ▪ VODKA ▪ OCELOT PAWS
CO-STARRING ▪ STUFFED PORCUPINE ▪ BOILED PEACOCK ▪ HORSERADISH ▪ CREAMED PEAS
MUSIC BY ▪ SQUID INK SACS ▪ SCREENPLAY BY ▪ POACHED OYSTERS ▪ ORIGINAL STORY BY ▪ MINCED COCKATOO
PRODUCED BY ▪ BLOOD OF A PIG AND VODKA ▪ DIRECTED BY ▪ BONELESS FISH

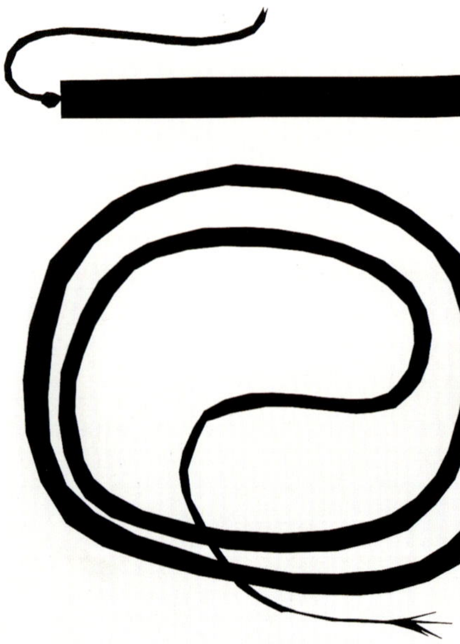

All You Need Is Love

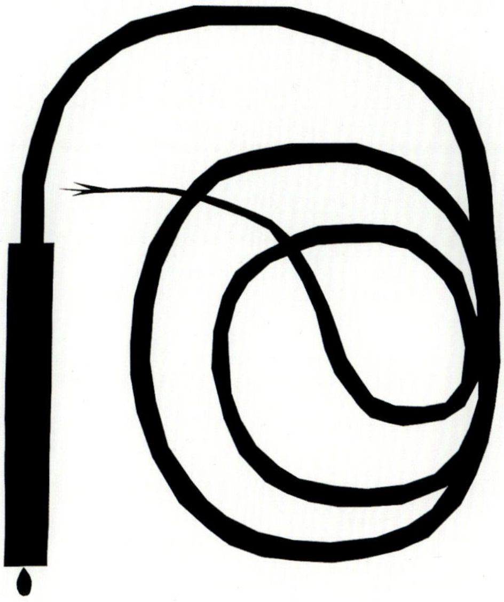

To Choose Wrongly A Career

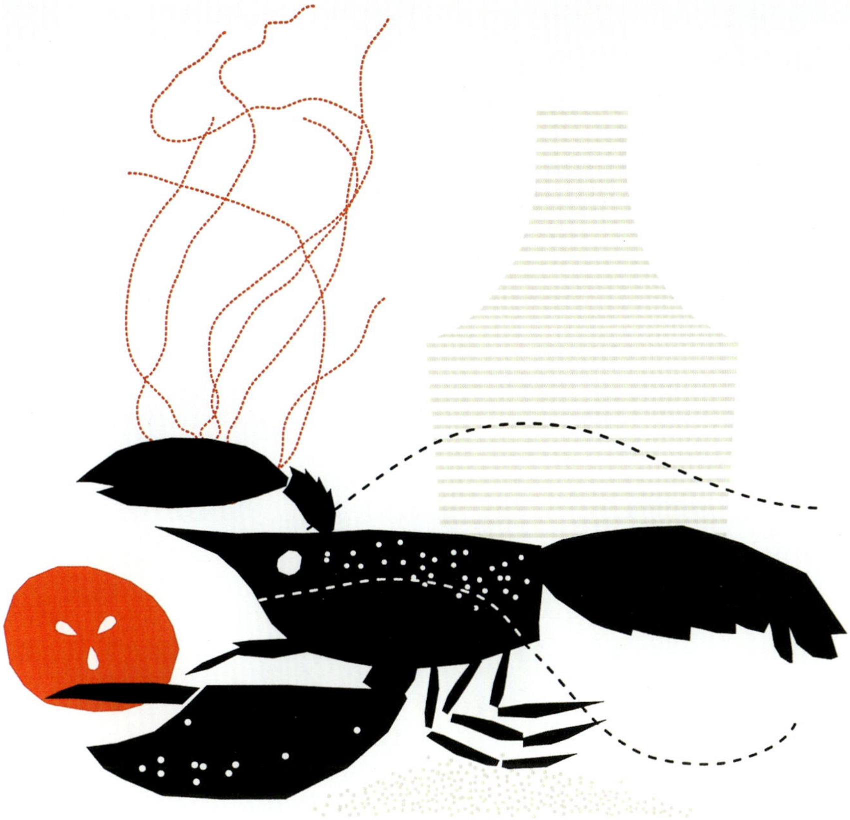

Vultures & Collectors

• PRESSED AGAINST THE WINDOW • PUSHED AGAINST THE TILE • PINNED TO THE FLOOR •
• BODY FOUND IN THE AFTERNOON • BRIGHT LIGHT ON AN UNMADE BED • CAT RESTS ON BACK •
• NEVER LIKED TO DANCE • DROVE INTO A PERSONAL WALL • NEVER LIKED JAZZ •

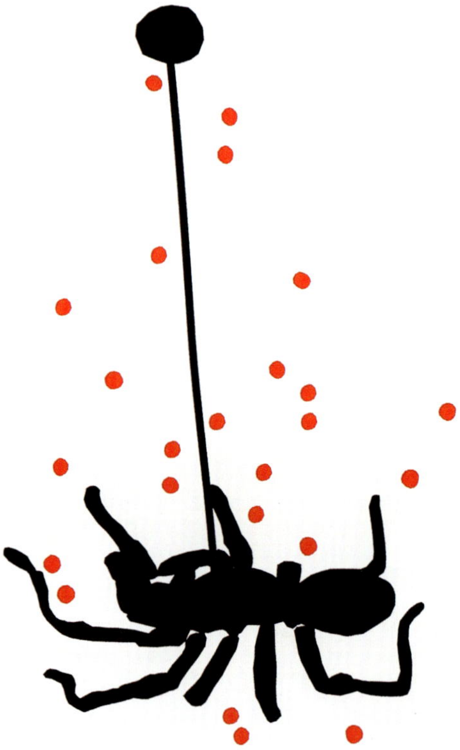

How It All Ends

• TUGGING AT YOUR BELT • BRACING YOURSELF FOR THE COLD • SENDING THE KIDS TO REHAB •
• FEAR STEERS THE METHOD • UNDERSTANDING REVENGE • EXPENSIVE SEXUAL RELATION • INEXPENSIVE SEXUAL RELATION •
• TOLD HIM WHERE TO PUT IT • LOST THE POINT • THE FORCE OF SAYING NO • THE FORCE OF REGRET •

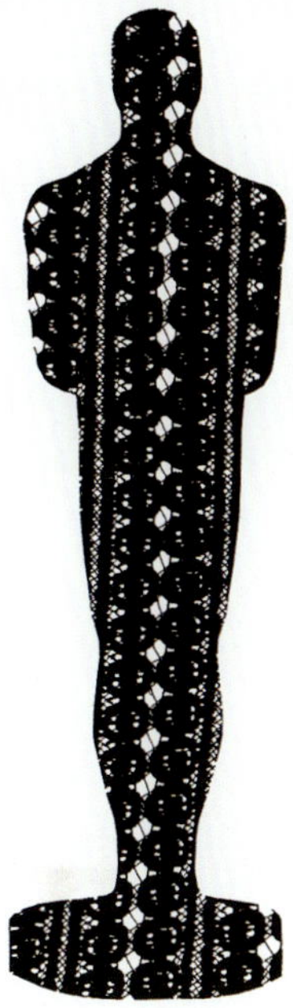

A Lot Like Trash

• AVOIDING FAME • DODGING ACCOUNTABILITY • CROWD PLEASING TEST DRIVE • PRETENDING TO CARE •
• A CONSERVATIVE VERSION OF RADICAL • A RADICAL VERSION OF CONSERVATIVE •
• WATCHING IT ALL HAPPEN • ANTICIPATING THE BACKLASH • EVEN PARANOID PEOPLE HAVE ENEMIES •

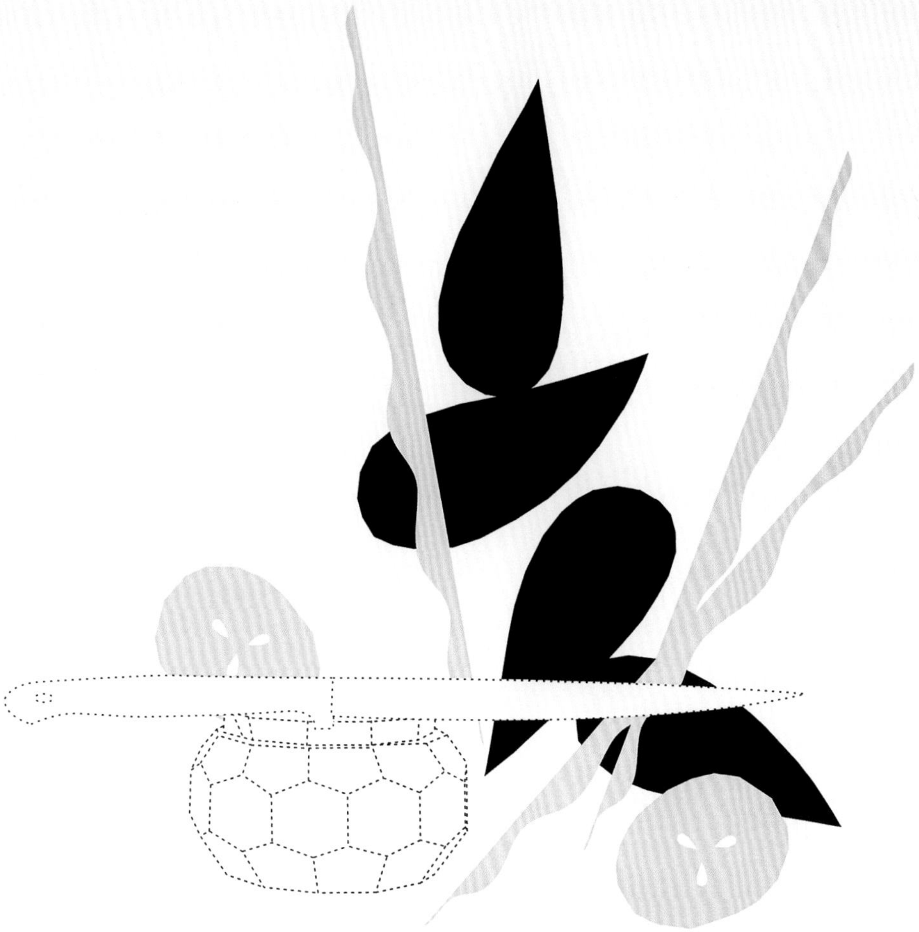

Less Than Sympathetic

• DISAPPOINTMENT IS SPECIFIC • ITS TARGET PERSONAL • A PLAGUE OF PERSECUTION FANTASIES •
• YOUR SUSPICION PALES • YOUR WORST FEAR REALIZED • THE MISFORTUNES OF VIRTUE • DECISION TO STOP •
• NOT A POET • PUSHED IN FRONT OF TRAFFIC • CREATING A FEELING OF VACANCY IN OTHERS •

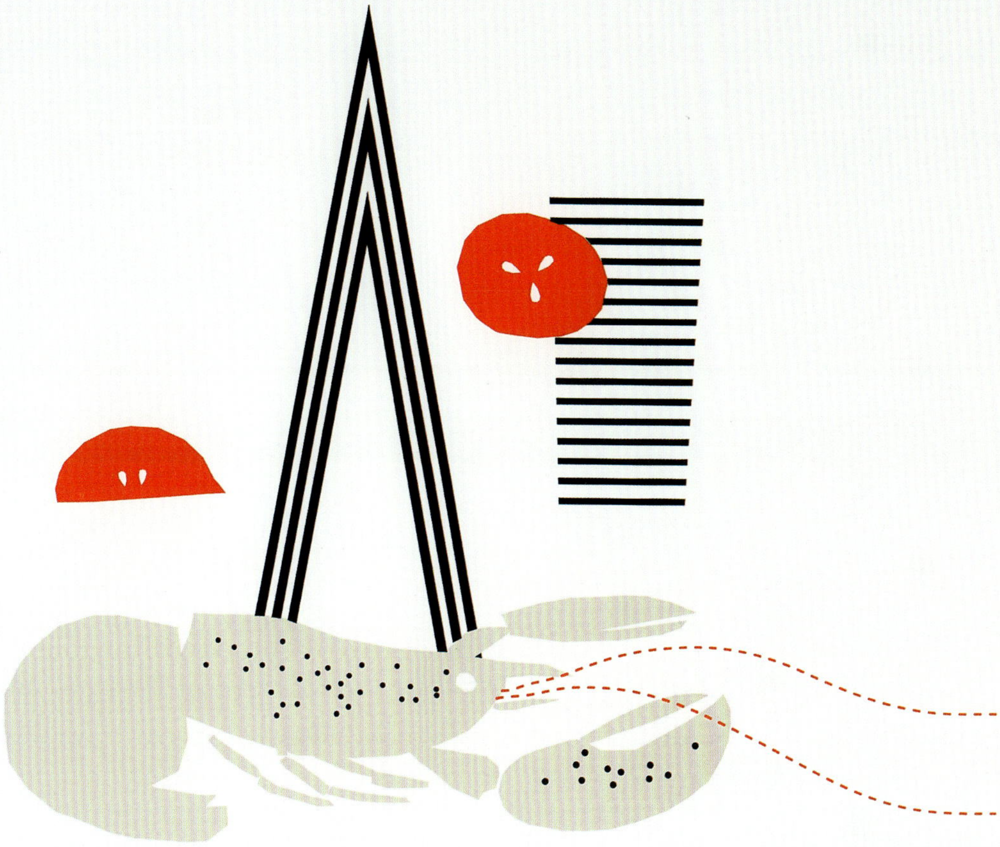

The Price of Admission

• THIS IS HOW IT ENDS • THAT WAS HOW IT ENDED • THE APOCALYPSE IS A JOKE •
• THE LIFE SPAN OF THE WORLD DOES NOT MIRROR HUMAN LIFE • ROCKS IN MOTION • SEAS OF DEAD FISH •
• ANIMALS IN ZOOS DIE DIFFERENTLY THAN IN THE WILD • NEVER THOUGHT YOU HAD IT IN YOU •

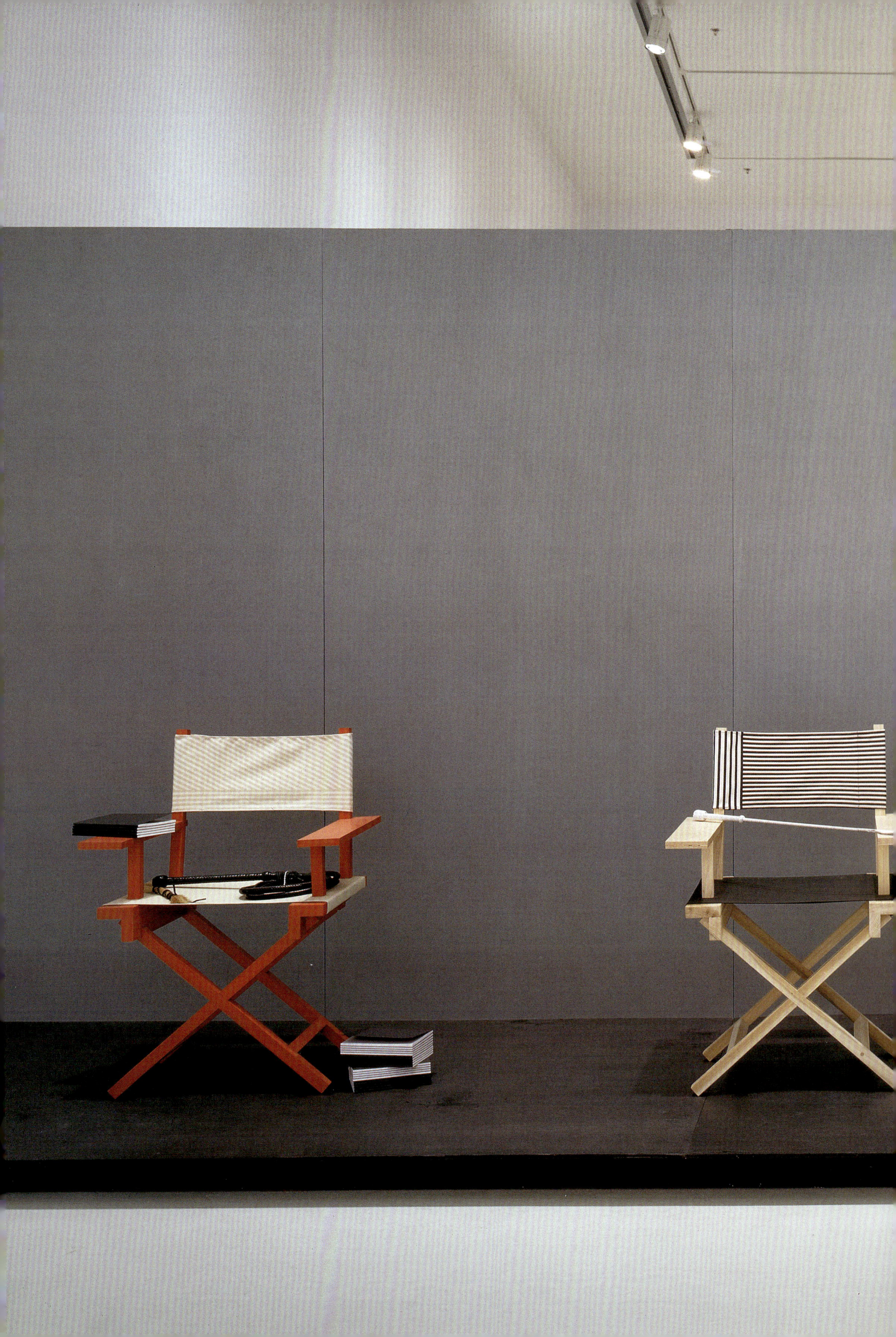

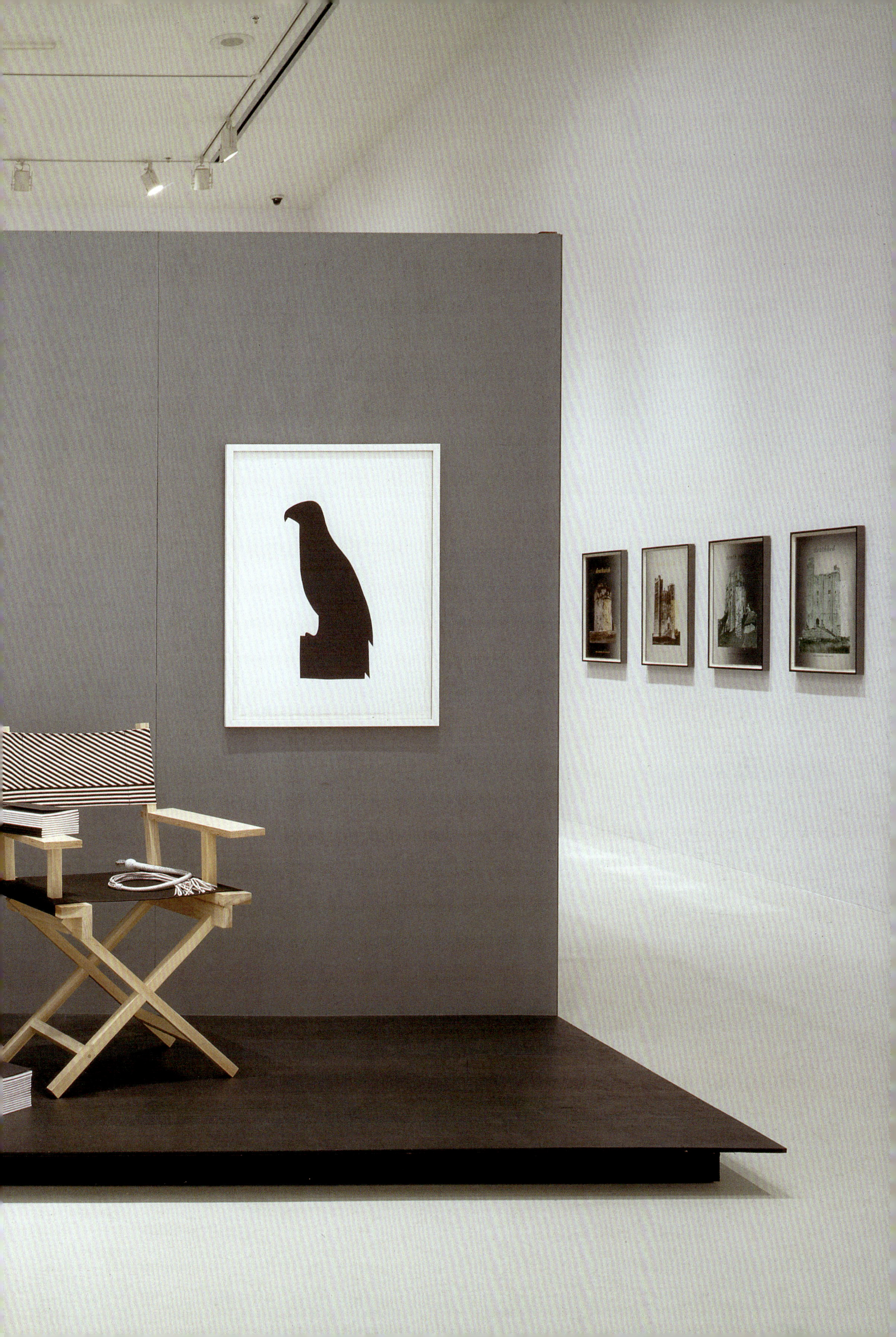

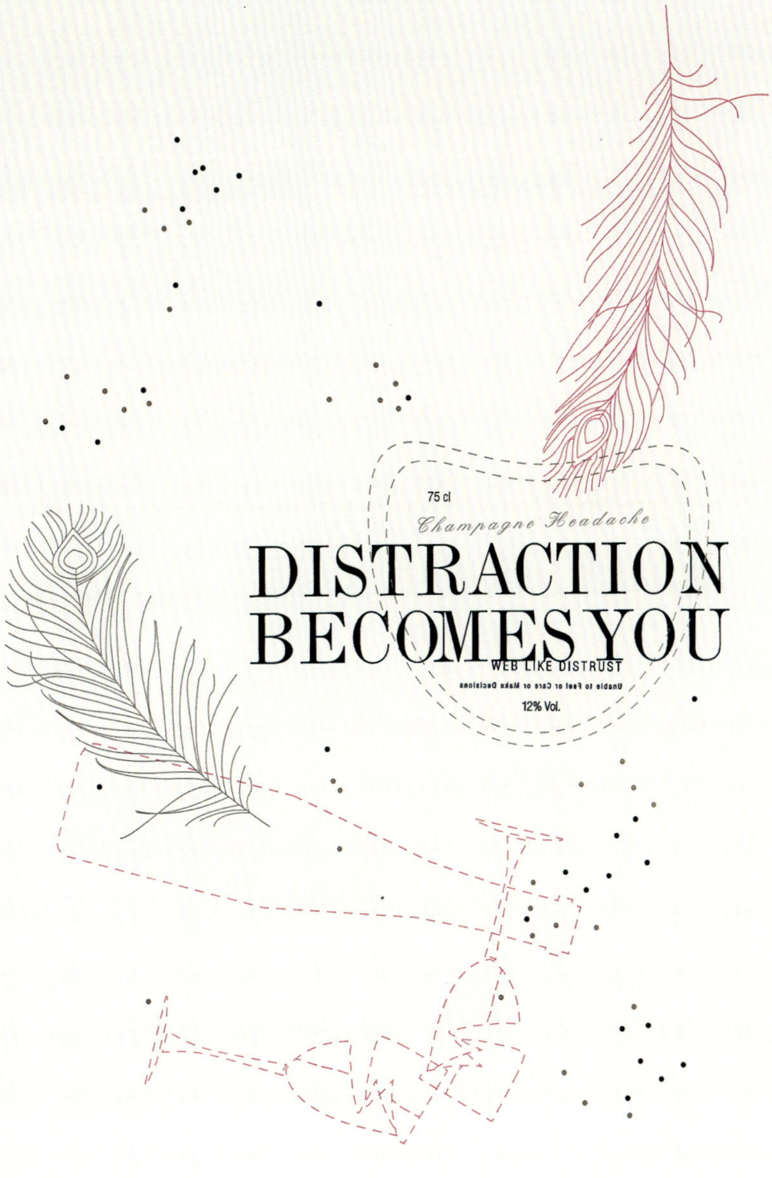
75 cl
Champagne Headache
DISTRACTION
BECOMES YOU
WEB LIKE DISTRUST
Unable to Feel or Care or Make Decisions
12% Vol.

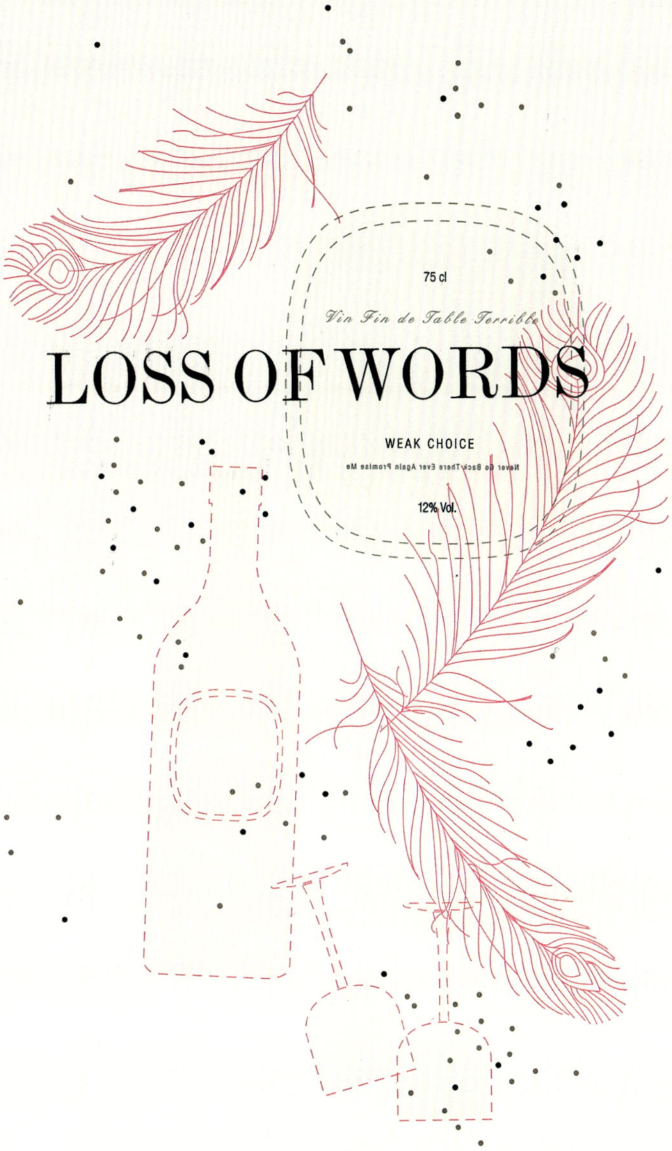
75 cl
Vin Fin de Table Terrible
LOSS OF WORDS
WEAK CHOICE
Never Go Back There Ever Again Promise Me
12% Vol.

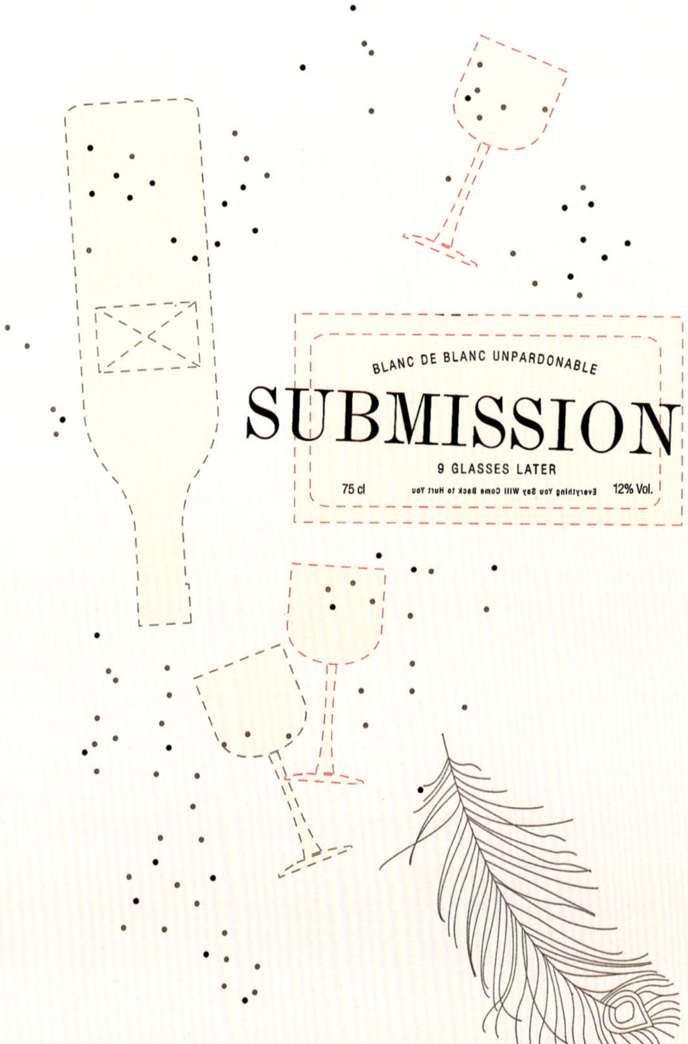
BLANC DE BLANC UNPARDONABLE
SUBMISSION
9 GLASSES LATER
75 cl
Everything You Say Will Come Back to Hurt You
12% Vol.

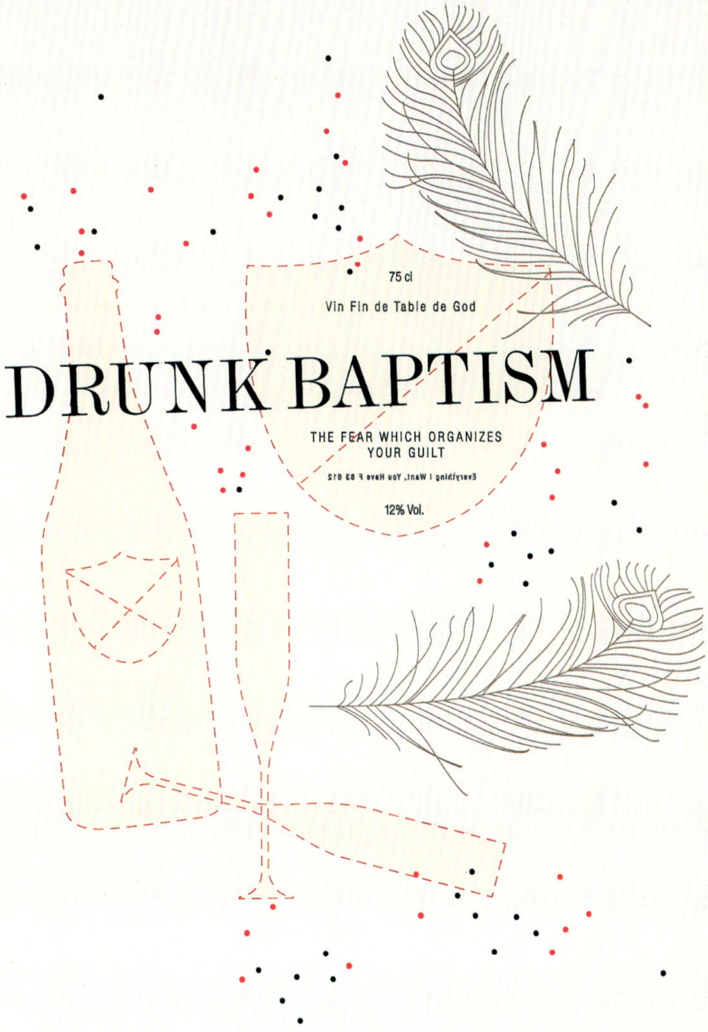
75 cl
Vin Fin de Table de God
DRUNK BAPTISM
THE FEAR WHICH ORGANIZES
YOUR GUILT
Everything I Want, You Have F 83 612
12% Vol.

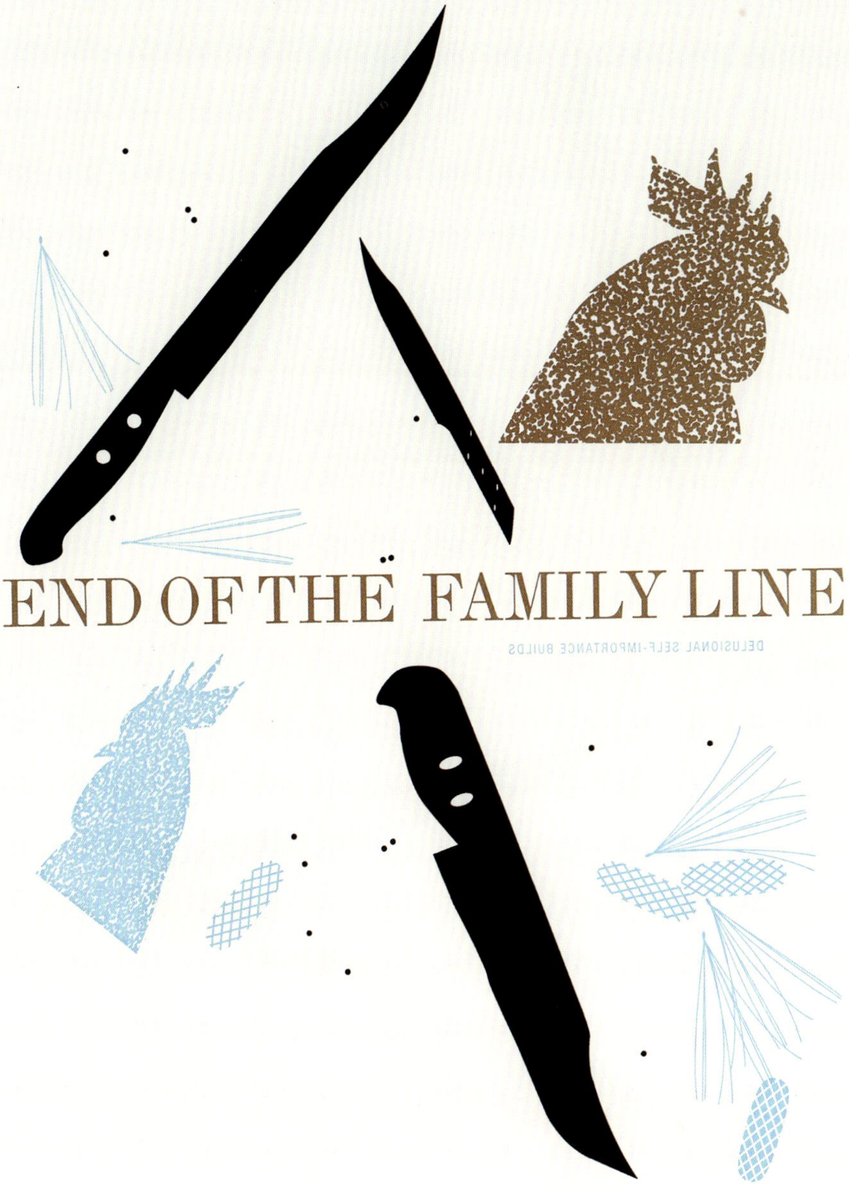
END OF THE FAMILY LINE
DELUSIONAL SELF-IMPORTANCE BUILDS

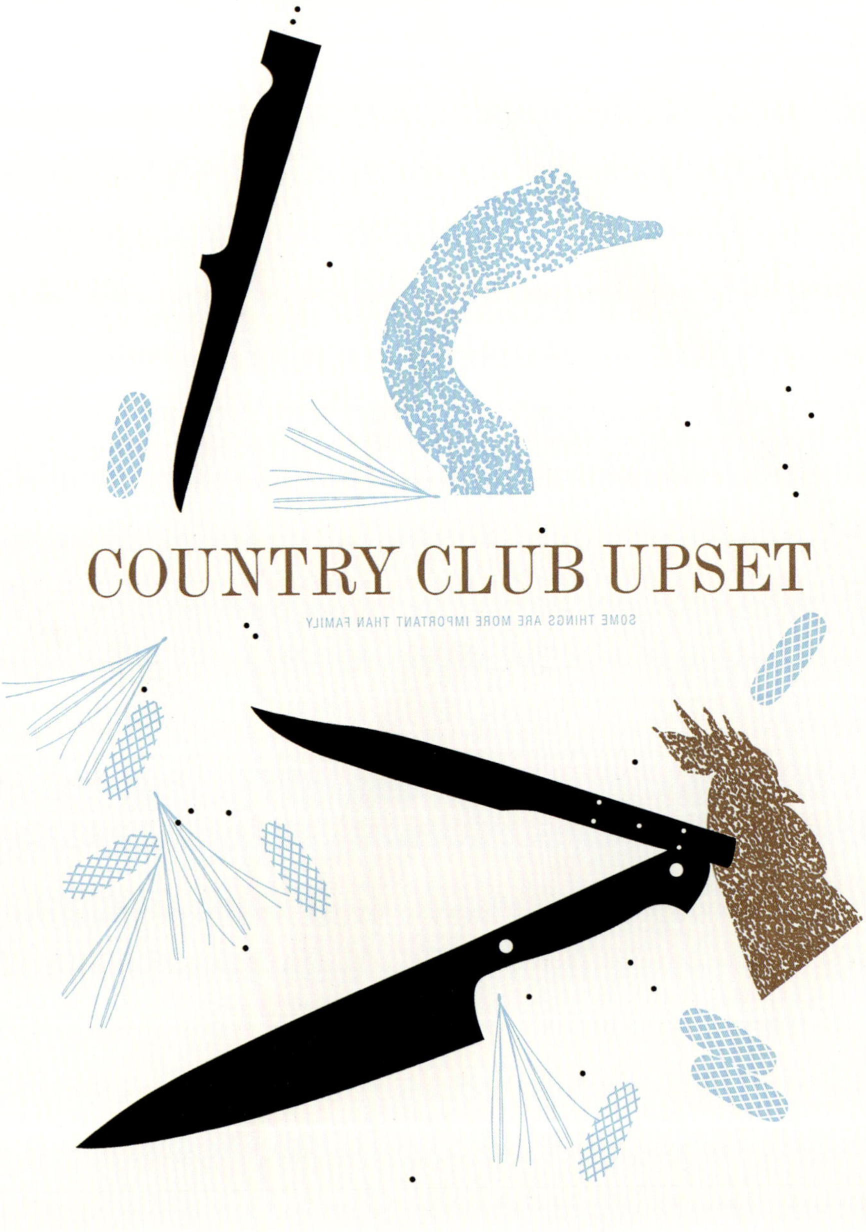
COUNTRY CLUB UPSET
SOME THINGS ARE MORE IMPORTANT THAN FAMILY

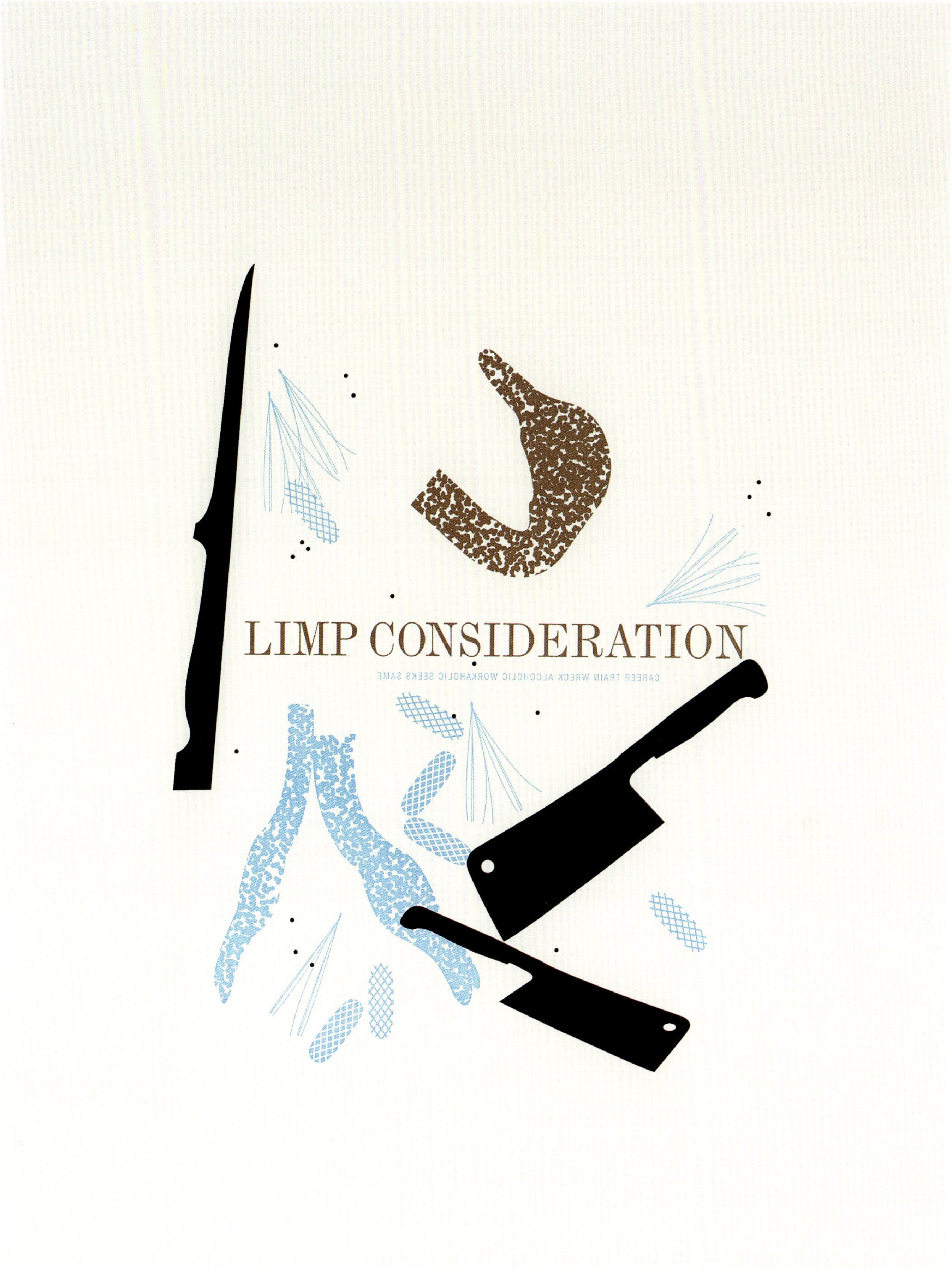
LIMP CONSIDERATION
CAREER TRAIN WRECK ALCOHOLIC WORKAHOLIC SEEKS SAME

DISAPPOINTED CRITIC
DIET PILL PARANOIA & PLASTIC TROPHIES

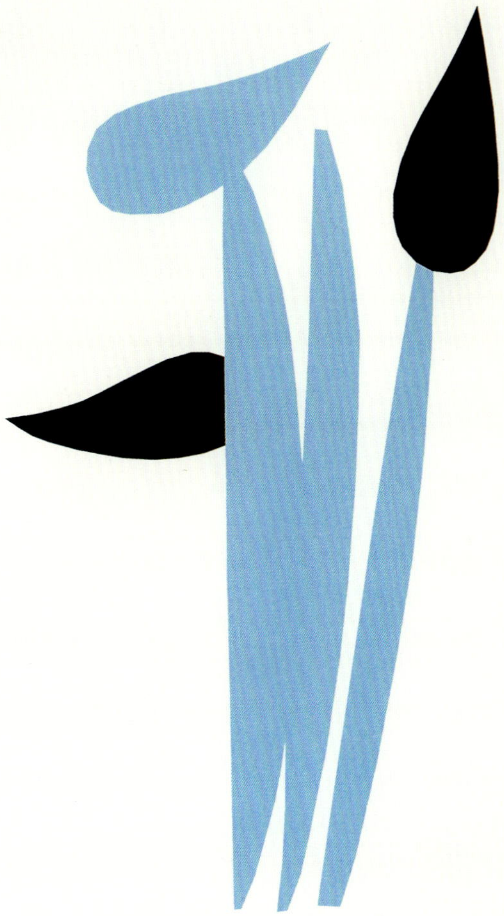

Hair of the Dog

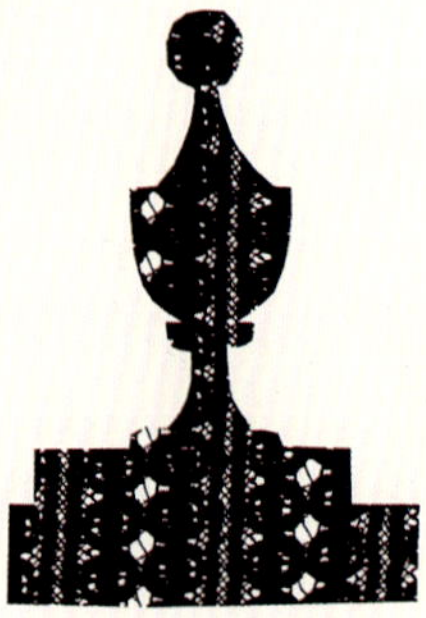

• WALL TO WALL MIRRORS IN A PRIVATE BATHROOM AT A PARTY YOU NEED TO LEAVE •
• PALM TREES BRUSH THE WINDOW • OUTSIDE THE SOUND OF INSECTS • THE CREDIT CARD DOESN'T HAVE YOUR NAME ON IT •
• SLIDE THE MIRROR RIGHT • SCAN THE PRESCRIPTIONS • SLIDE THE MIRROR LEFT • NOTE THE MOUTHWASH & BAND AIDS •
• AN ASHED CIGARETTE INSIDE A FORTY FIVE DOLLAR SCENTED CANDLE • BLACK SOAP IN THE SHAPE OF A DOG • PERFUME & POWDER BOTTLES •
• LOOK AT YOUR GRAY FACE • RUN YOUR HANDS UNDER COLD WATER • RUN YOUR TOUNGE OVER YOUR TEETH • TASTE BLOOD •
• BREATHE IN AND FLINCH • YOUR COCK NOW HALF ITS SIZE • SWALLOW BITTER PLEGHM • FIGHT THE PANIC • FIGHT THE NAUSEA •
• THIS ISN'T PART OF YOUR JOB DESCRIPTION • THIS ISN'T THE WAY IT ENDS • THIS IS THE AWFUL LAST OF IT •
• HOLD THE SINK ON YOUR WAY TO THE FLOOR • LAY YOUR HEAD IN THE PISS SOAKED RUG • TRY TO FOCUS • WAVES OF HEAT & PRESSURE •
• SOMEONE IS KNOCKING • EVERYONE IS LAUGHING • WISH THAT CANDLE WAS OUT •

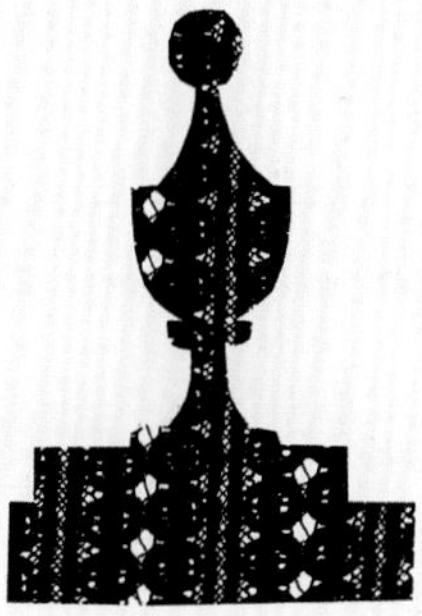

• ONE SEVENTEEN A.M. YOU EXCUSE YOURSELF FROM THE TABLE AT A RESTAURANT YOU CAN NOT AFFORD •
• SAFE IN THE STALL • YOU REACH BACK AND FLIP THE LATCH • ALREADY ANXIOUS ABOUT LEAVING •
• YOUR EXPOSED BACK STICKS AGAINST THE GRAY METAL DIVIDER • YOUR HEELS REST ON NOTHING SOLID •
• YOUR NEW SHOES ARE NO CONSOLATION • THE DAY'S MANICURE REFLECTS YOUR BLACK HOLE EYES ON YOUR BLUE NECK •
• BREATHE IN • YOU CAN'T FEEL ANY AIR • BREATHE IN • IS YOUR HEART EVEN WORKING • YOUR PULSE ERRATIC AND FAST •
• WHEN THEY SAID "THAT JOKE ISN'T FUNNY ANYMORE," WERE THEY REFERRING TO YOU •
• YOU SHOULD DRINK MORE WATER • NEVER LEARN • NEVER AGAIN • YOU SHOULD HAVE STAYED HOME •
• TRY TO SIT BUT THERE IS NO BENEFIT • YOUR HANDS TOUCH THE COLD WET PORCELAIN • DROP YOUR NECK FORWARD •
• FEEL YOUR HEART SKIP • YOUR HAIR MAKES A CANOPY •

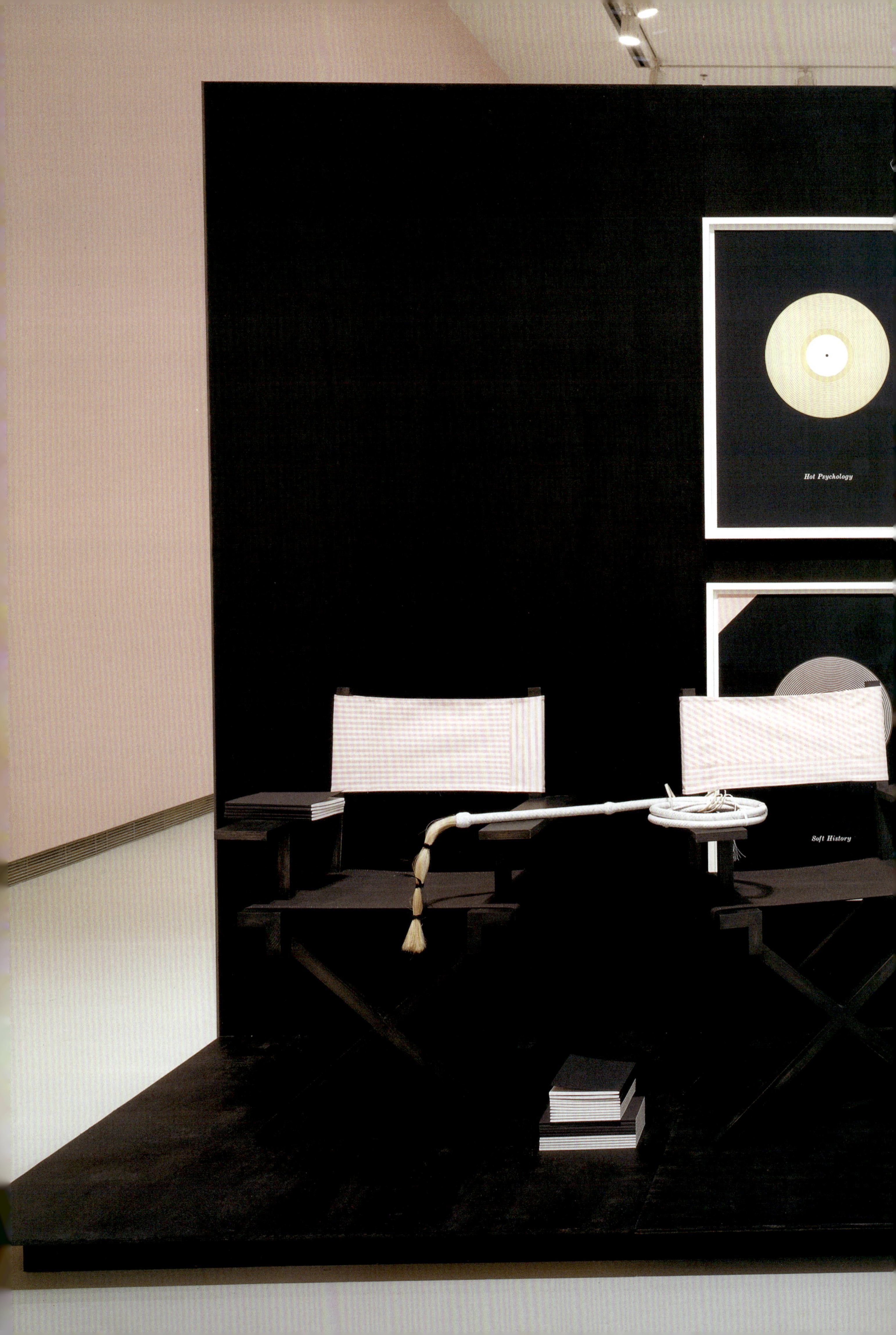
Hot Psychology
Soft History

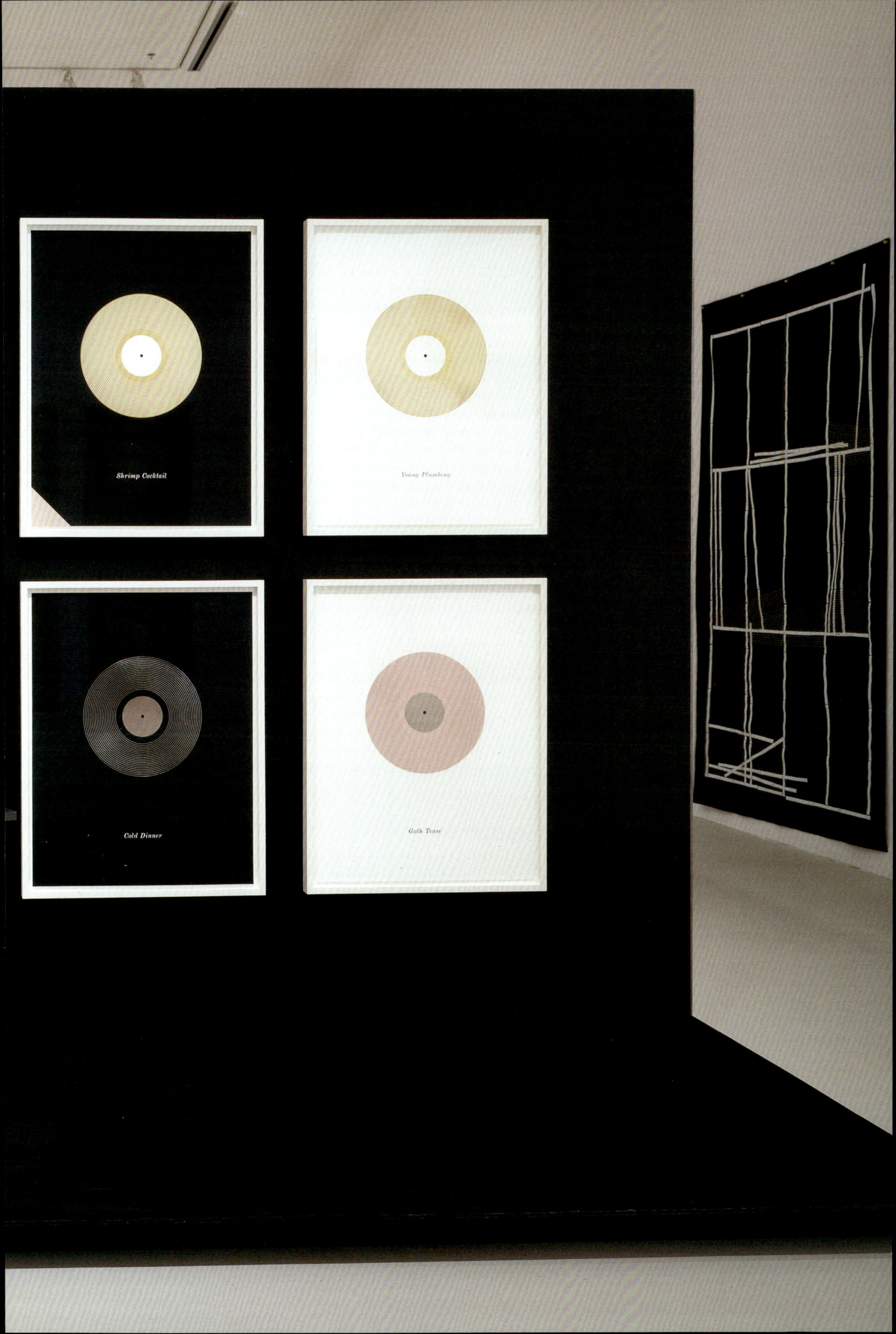
Shrimp Cocktail
Young Plumbing
Cold Dinner
Goth Tease

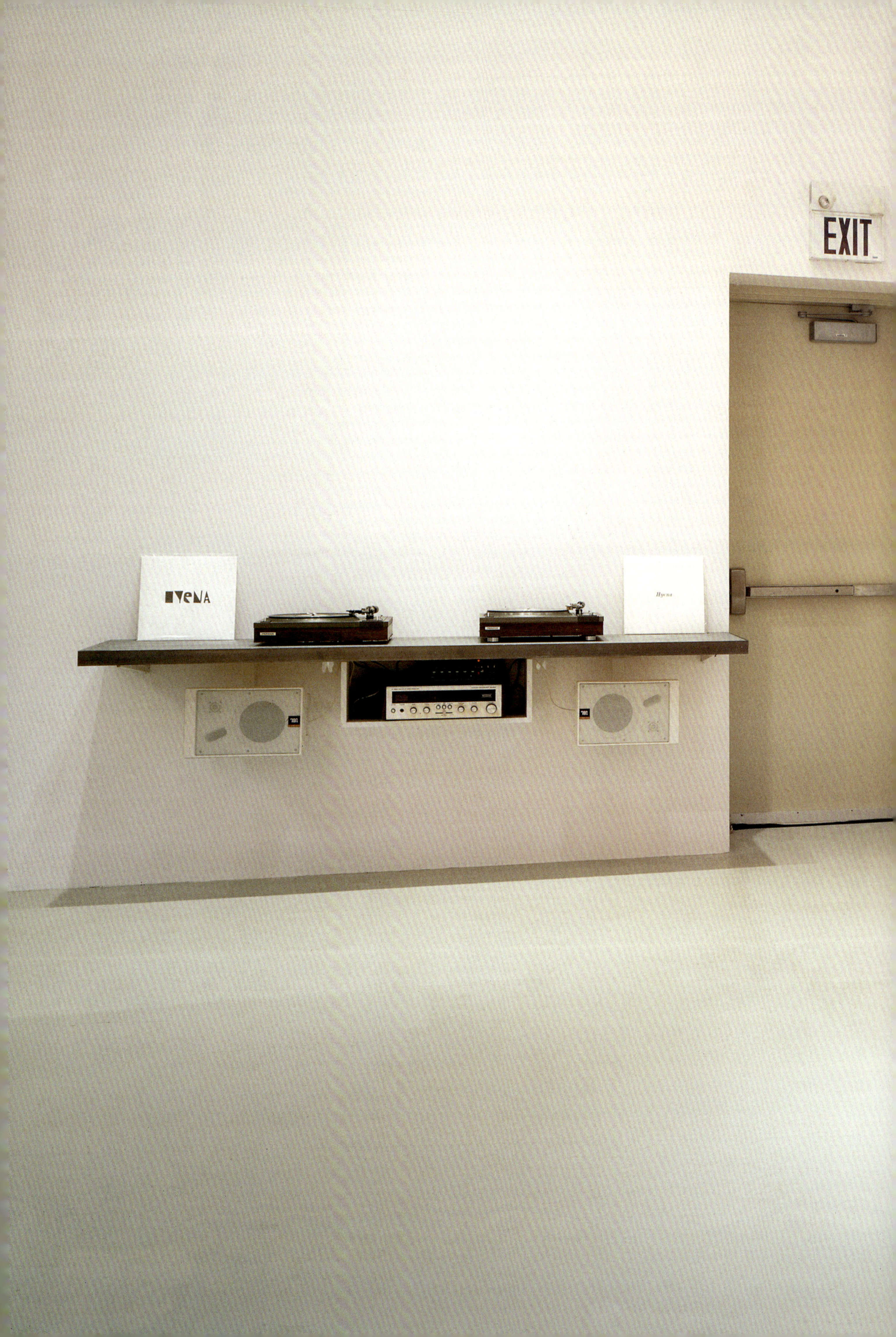
EXIT
HYENA
Hyena

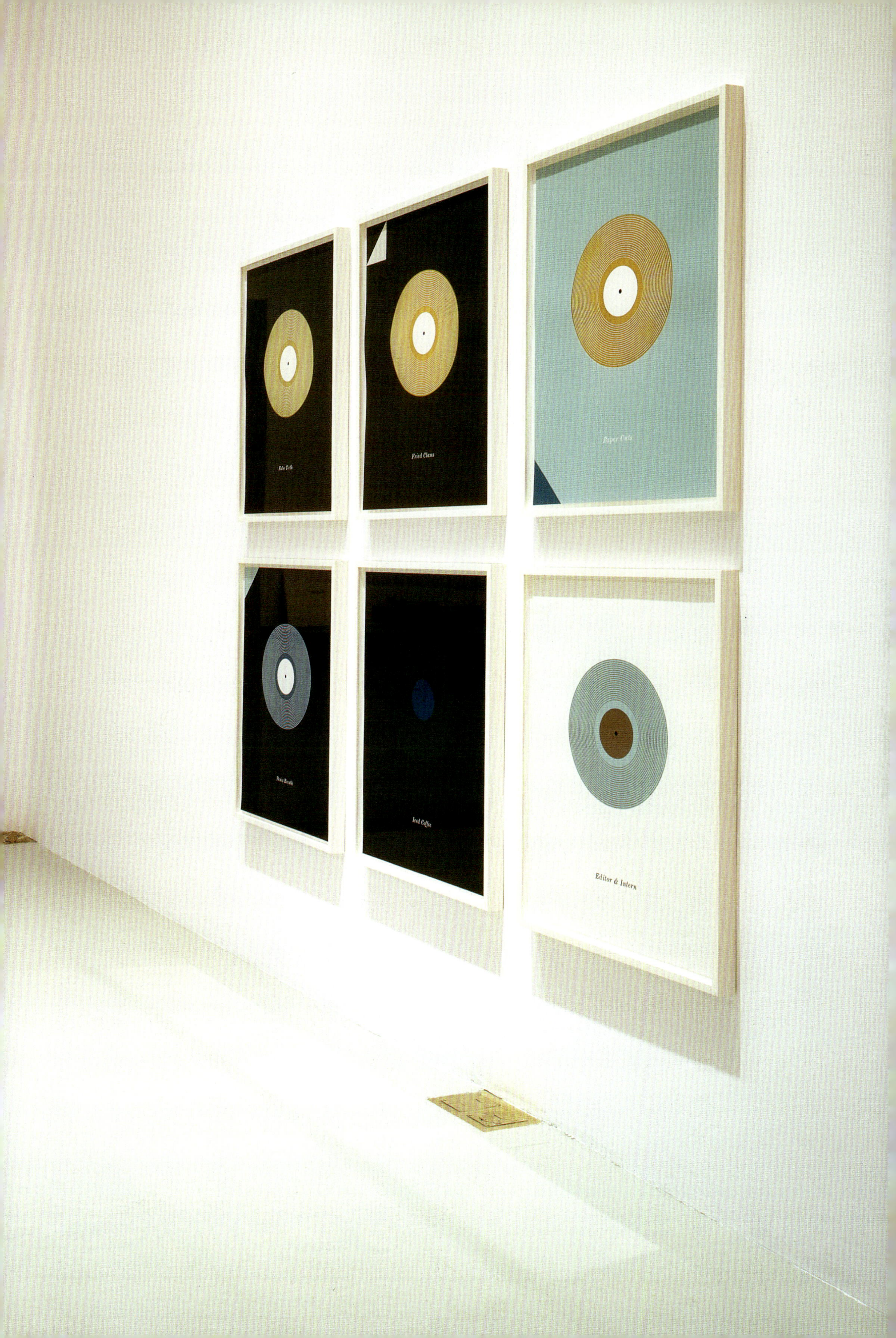
False Teeth
Fried Clams
Paper Cuts
Iced Coffee
Editor & Intern

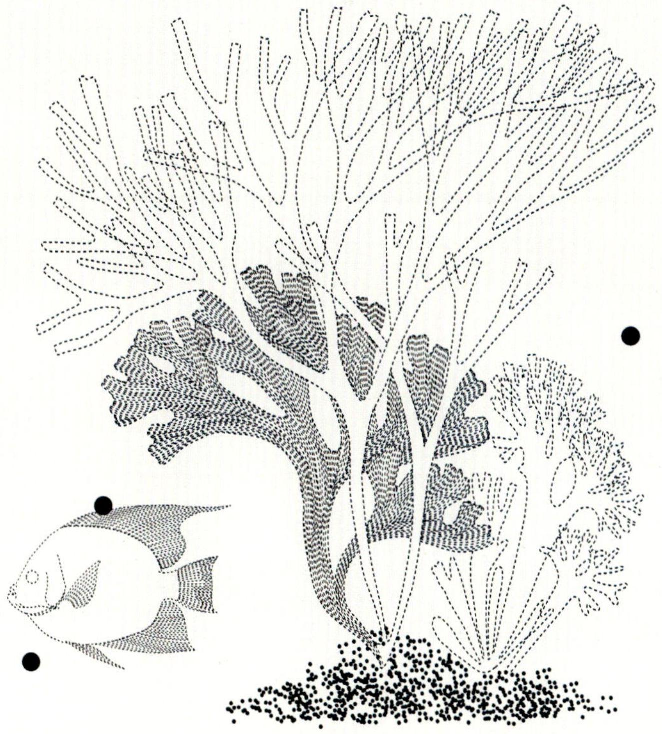

Fatal Career Misstep

• DERIVATIVE & MAGNETIC PAINTING • YOUR SEXUAL HISTORY • OTHER PEOPLES' MONEY • SHELVED FILM •
• HEROIN TASTE TEST • TEMPERED DISCIPLINE • ONE WEEKS PAY IN ONE NIGHT • TOTALLY GREAT & TOTALLY TRUE •
• FLOOD OF REGRET • FURIOUS FOSTER PARENT • HORSING AROUND IN BED • YOUNG PLUMBING •

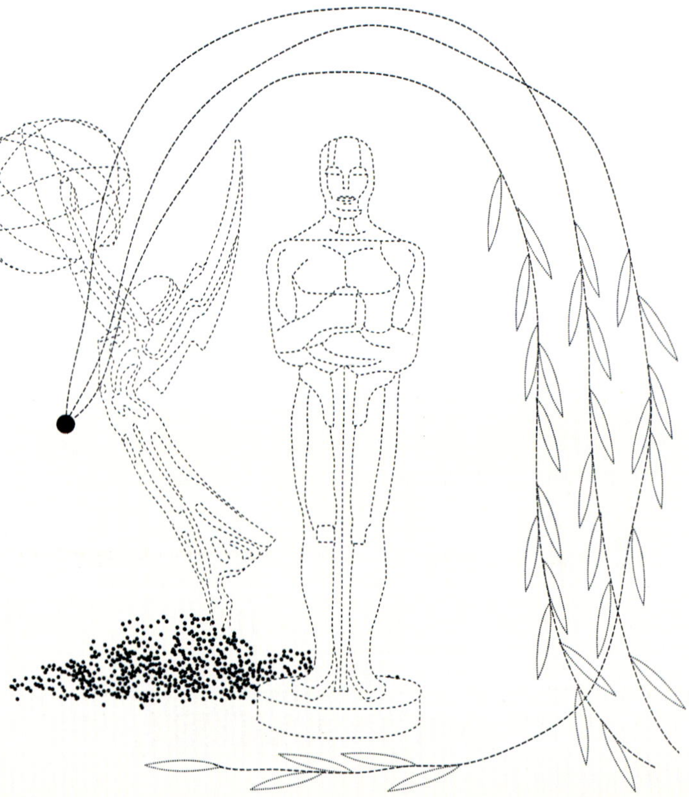

Premature Ejaculation

• SUPERFICIAL BURNS SURFACE • POLICE OFFICER GIVING UP • EUROPEAN FURNITURE SHOWROOM • PATIENT HAND JOB •
• ROLE PLAYING HYENA • PATTERNS OF ABUSE • PALTRY TEMPTATION & AMBIVALENT MAKE OUT • SUCCESSFUL EVENT WITH VODKA •
• STANDARD TREATMENT • WEAKENED RESOLVE • TOKEN ADDICT • FLUSHED SCREENPLAY • VAGUE TUTOR •

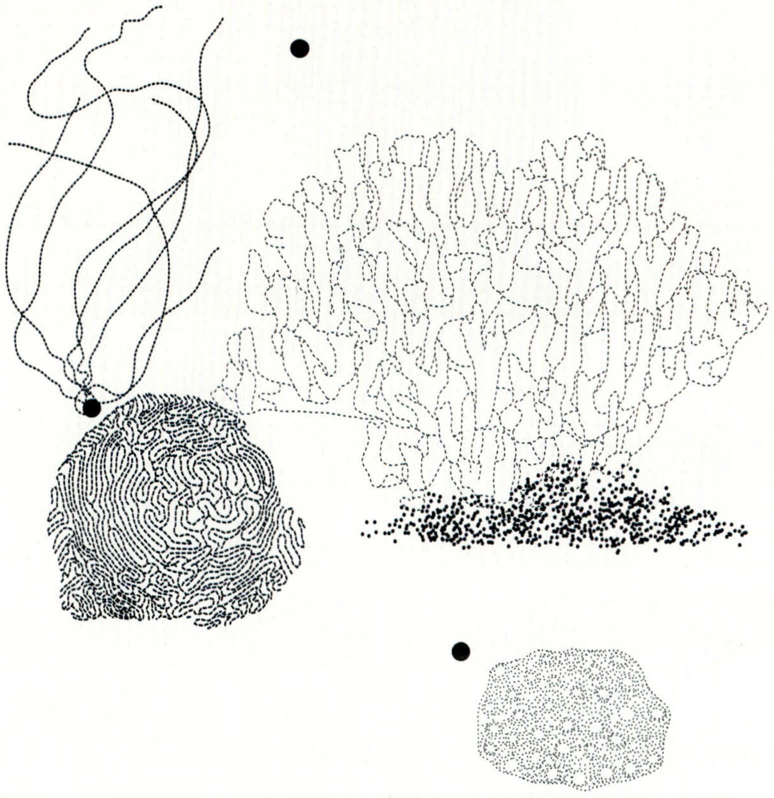

Belligerent Euphoria

• THE PASSIVE ART OF COMPLAINING • THE TIME BETWEEN SEIZURES • A PSYCHOLOGICAL BEACHHEAD •
• STEAMING WET PANT MEAT • APOLOGETIC FANS, FANATICS & FREAKS • SEVERED HANDS OF THE HUNTED • CANNIBAL DELICACIES •
• LIMP ATTEMPT • HAWKISH HOSTILE PUPPET • DETACHED PARENTS & DIPSOMANIACAL PIONEERS • VULNERABLE SOLDIER •

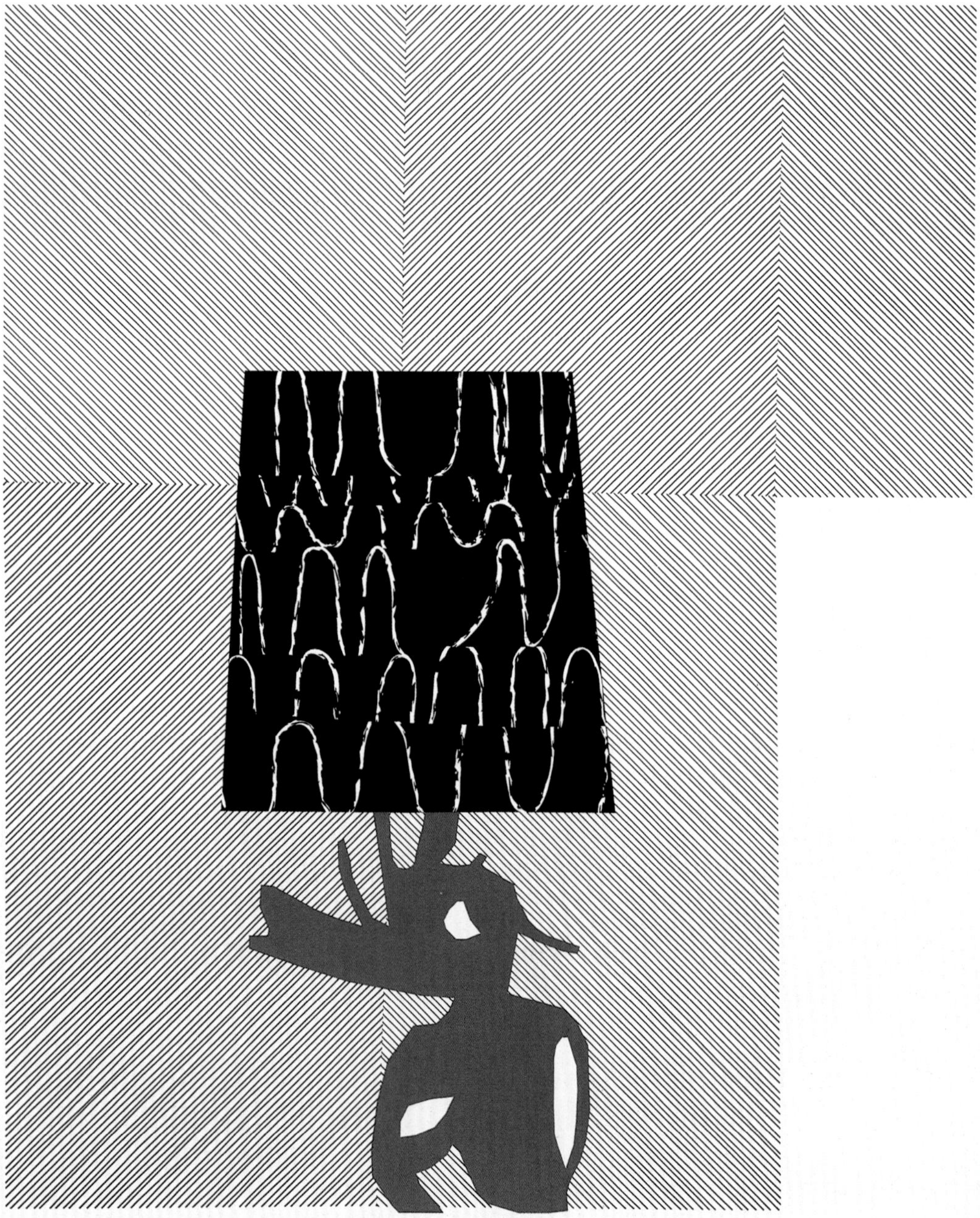

A Very Upsetting First Novel

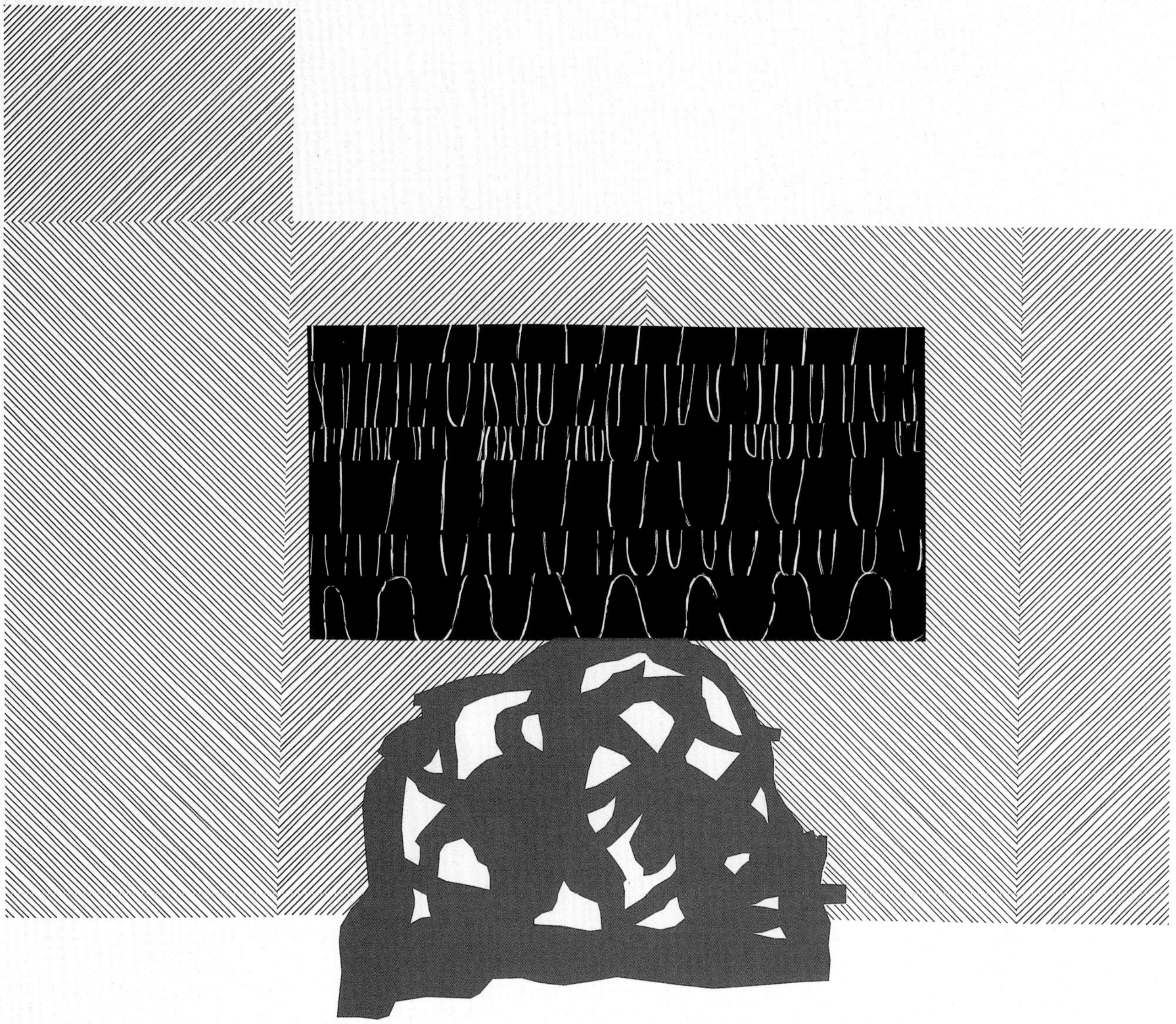

Pushing the Blade in Deeper

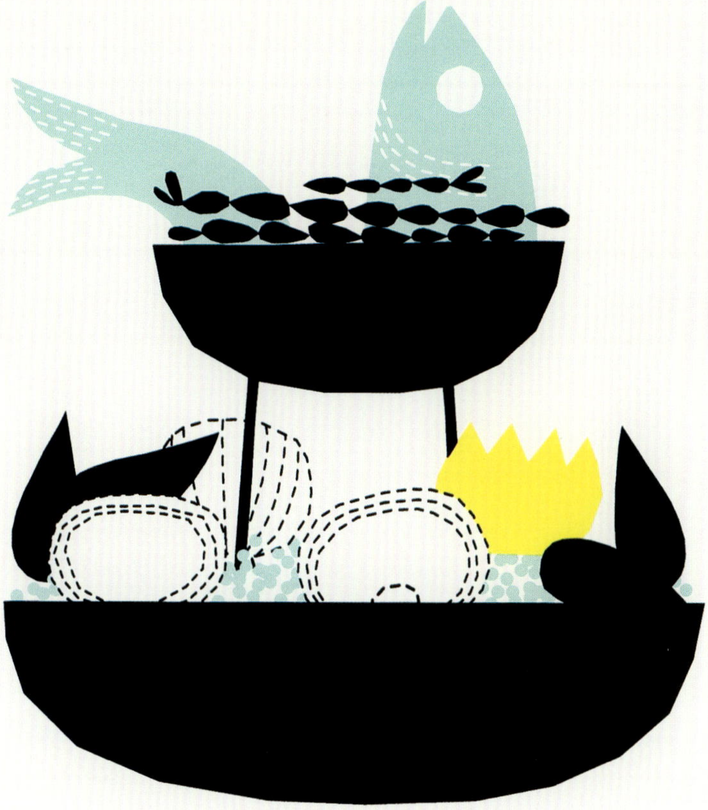

Compliance & Resentment

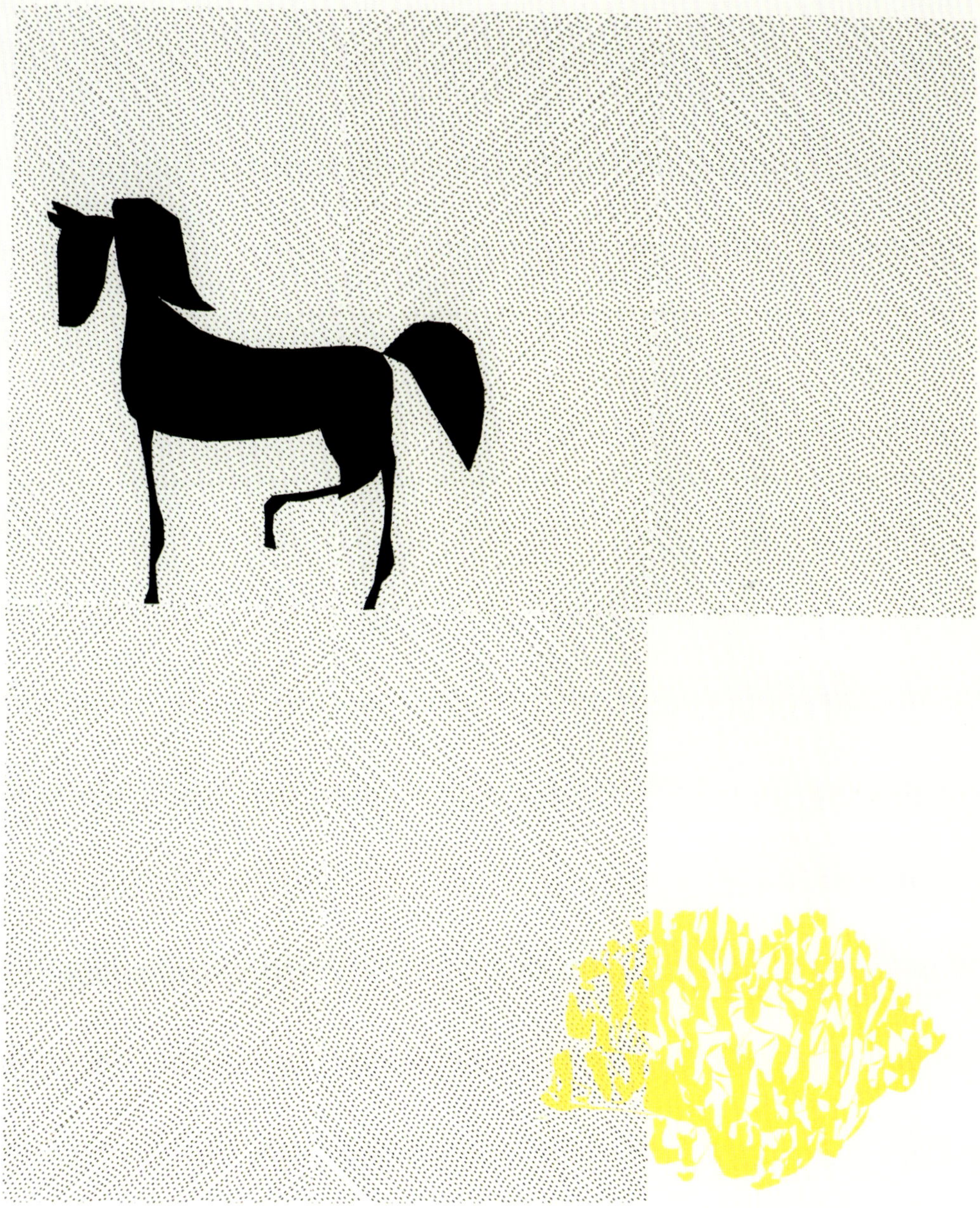

Performance Anxiety

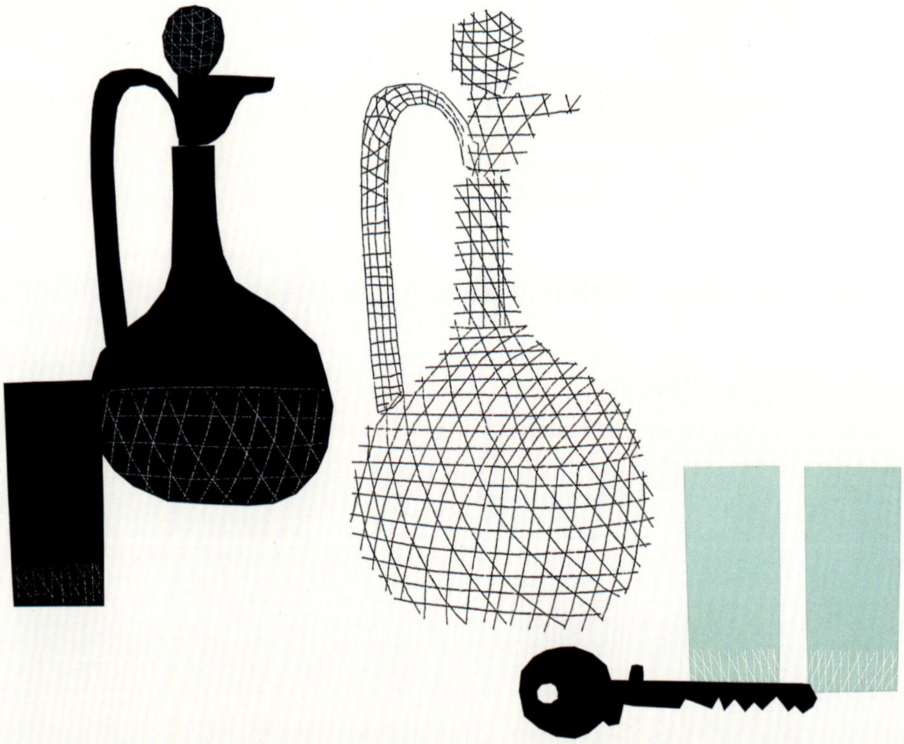

Holes in the Armor

• NIGHTSTAND OF SILVER PICTURE FRAMES & MEDICATION • IMPORTED OXYGEN & ANTIQUE ASHTRAYS •
• VEINS OVER BONES, UNDER LOOSE SKIN • A GLASS PARROT, A CRYSTAL PAPERWEIGHT, A DECORATIVE INKWELL • MORE GHOST STORY THAN NOVEL •
• A GRAMMAR TO REVEAL & A GRAMMAR TO DISGUISE CLASS • WE DIE BEFORE READING EVERYTHING WE THOUGHT WE WOULD •

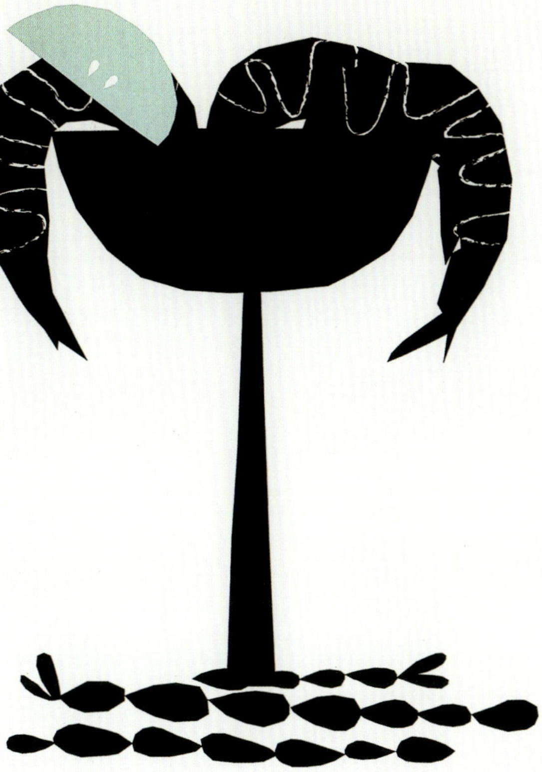

Slut Best Friend

• SPRAY IT WITH INSECTICIDE • CARPET IT WALL TO WALL • CUT IT IN HALF & HALF AGAIN • CALL IT A PLAN •
• GO TO RESTAURANTS FEW CAN AFFORD • COLLECT ART • BREED MINIATURE DOGS • BUY CLOTHES FEW COULD WEAR • ATTEMPT HARDCORE • BEG FOR ANOTHER CHANCE •
• ONCE EXOTIC NOW TEDIOUS • ALWAYS THE ALCOHOLIC • EVEN IN SOBRIETY • EVEN ON DAYS OFF • ESPECIALLY TONIGHT •

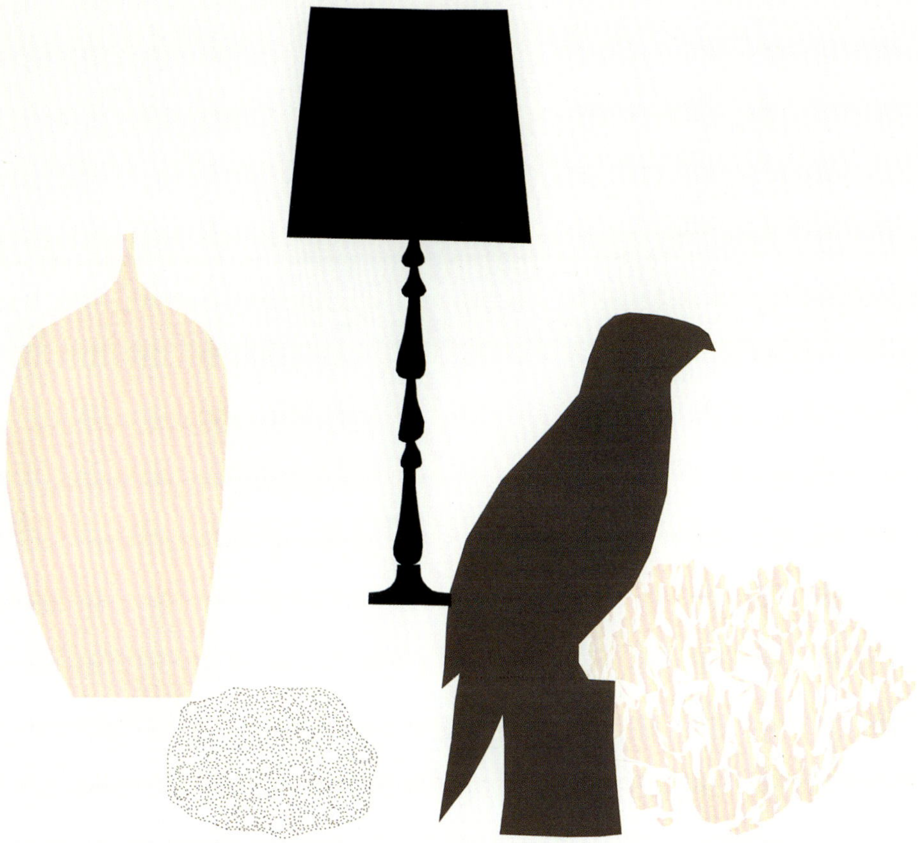

Star Becomes Co-Star

• A NURTURED ADDICTION • DISPOSABLE HEALTH • THE SETTING OF PERSONAL GOALS • THE BENDING OF WILL • THE FEEDING OF FEAR •
• JEWELRY MADE FROM ENDANGERED ANIMALS • GREAT HEAPS OF FLESH FROM THE SEA • WARM MEAT COVERED IN FLIES • THROATS FILLED WITH CONCRETE •
• THIS TRUTH HAS NO VALUE • THAT CRITICISM IS SELF SERVING • WOULDN'T YOU WERE A TEACHER • THOUGHT YOU WERE A PARENT •

Los Angeles

• WHEN THEY HIRED YOU THEY ASKED IF YOU WERE COMFORTABLE WITH IT • ASKED IF YOU'D DONE THIS BEFORE •
• ESTIMATE THE RISK, ACCEPT THE TERMS • AFRAID TO EVEN ANSWER THE PHONE • HIDE IN THE BATHROOM • PRETEND IT'S FUNNY - YOU MOVING HERE •
• BLAME YOURSELF • THREATEN OTHERS • TAKE UP SMOKING • STAY HOME TONIGHT •

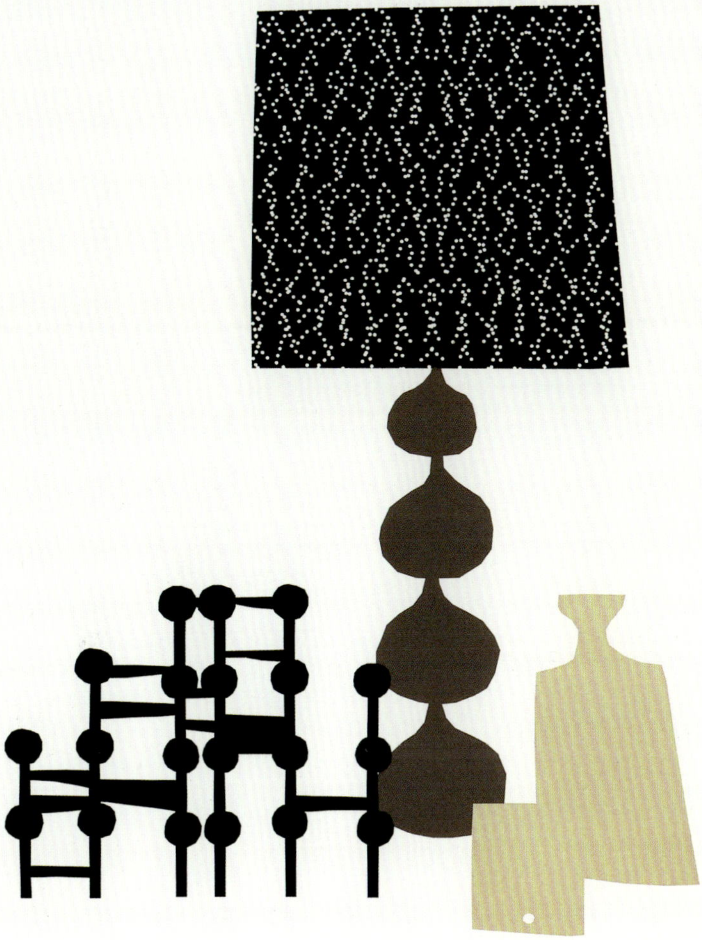

Crossing Swords

· I'M DRUNK · I'M WRITING THIS DRUNK · I CAN'T BEAR THE GUILT AND SHAME FOR WHAT I DID ·
· IT MIGHT NOT SEEM LIKE MUCH AFTER YOU READ THIS STORY · BUT IF YOU REALLY FOCUS ON WHAT IT MEANS TO DESTROY TWO COUPLES' LIVES YOU CAN BEGIN TO APPRECIATE HOW SAD IT ALL IS ·
· I'M SURE I'LL GET OVER IT · AND I'M SURE I'LL HAVE SEX AGAIN · BUT I HONESTLY FEEL LIKE I'VE RUINED SO MUCH RIGHT NOW · I'M TOTALLY DRUNK ·

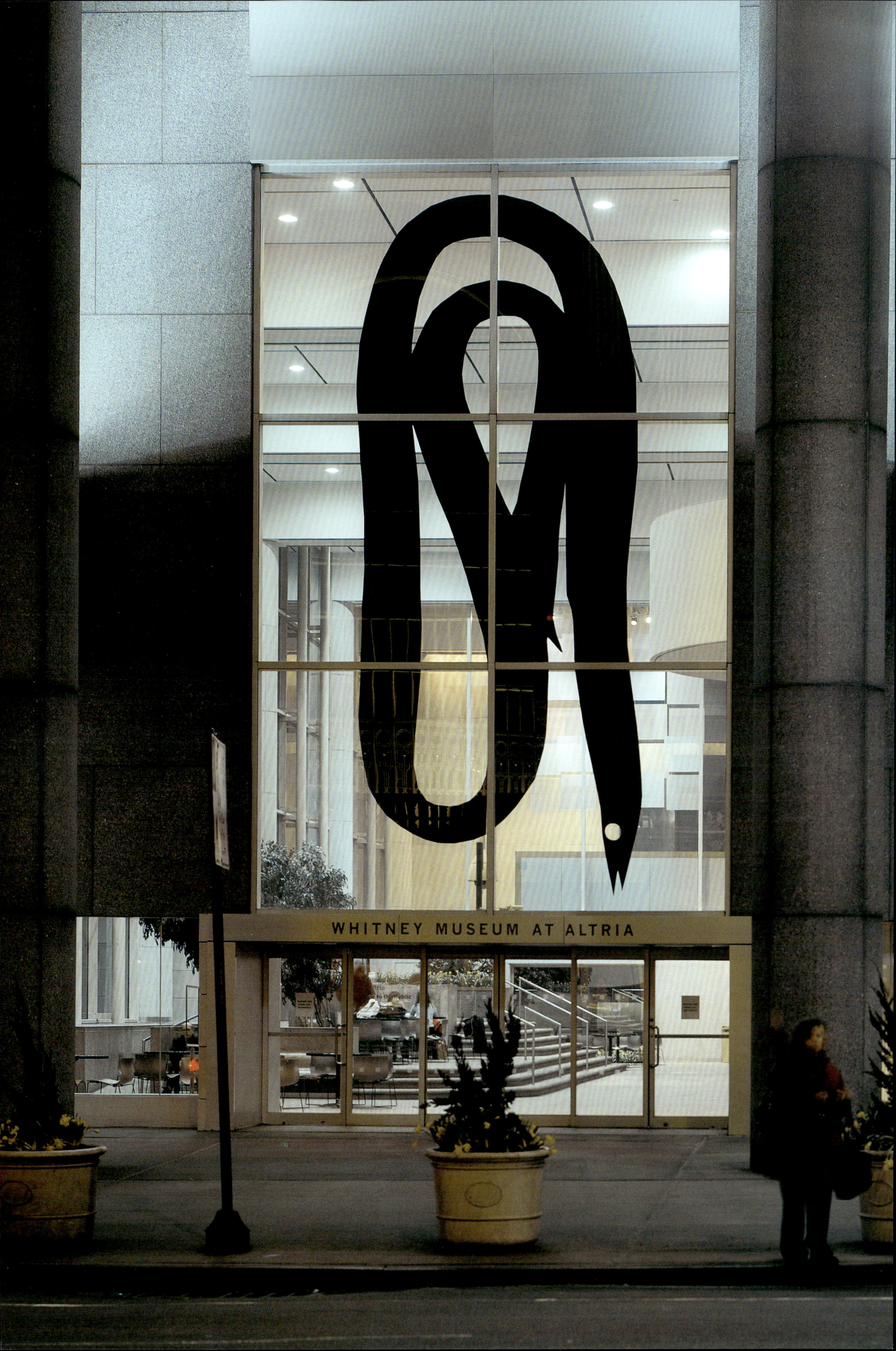
WHITNEY MUSEUM AT ALTRIA

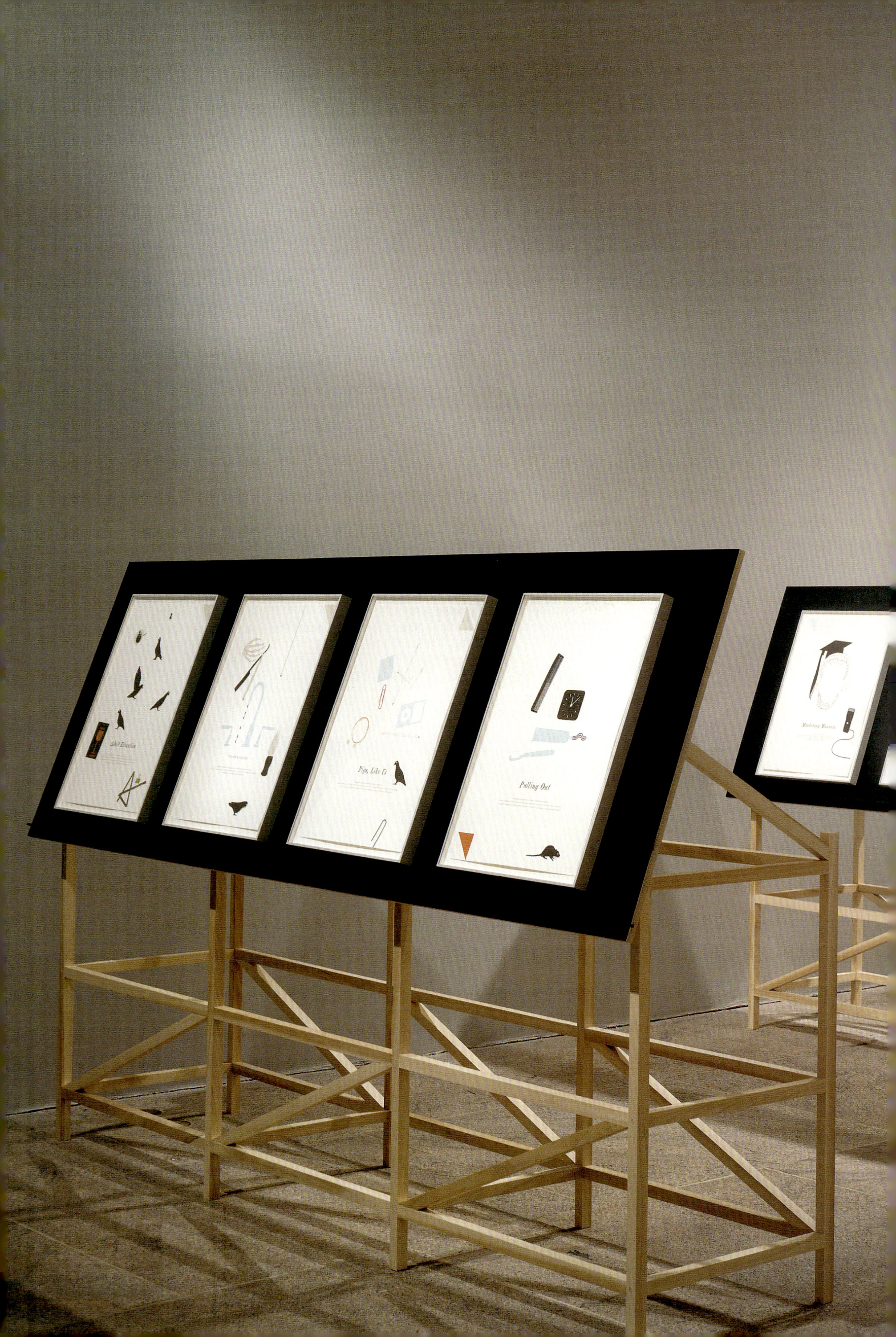
Adult Education
Pigs, Like Us
Pulling Out

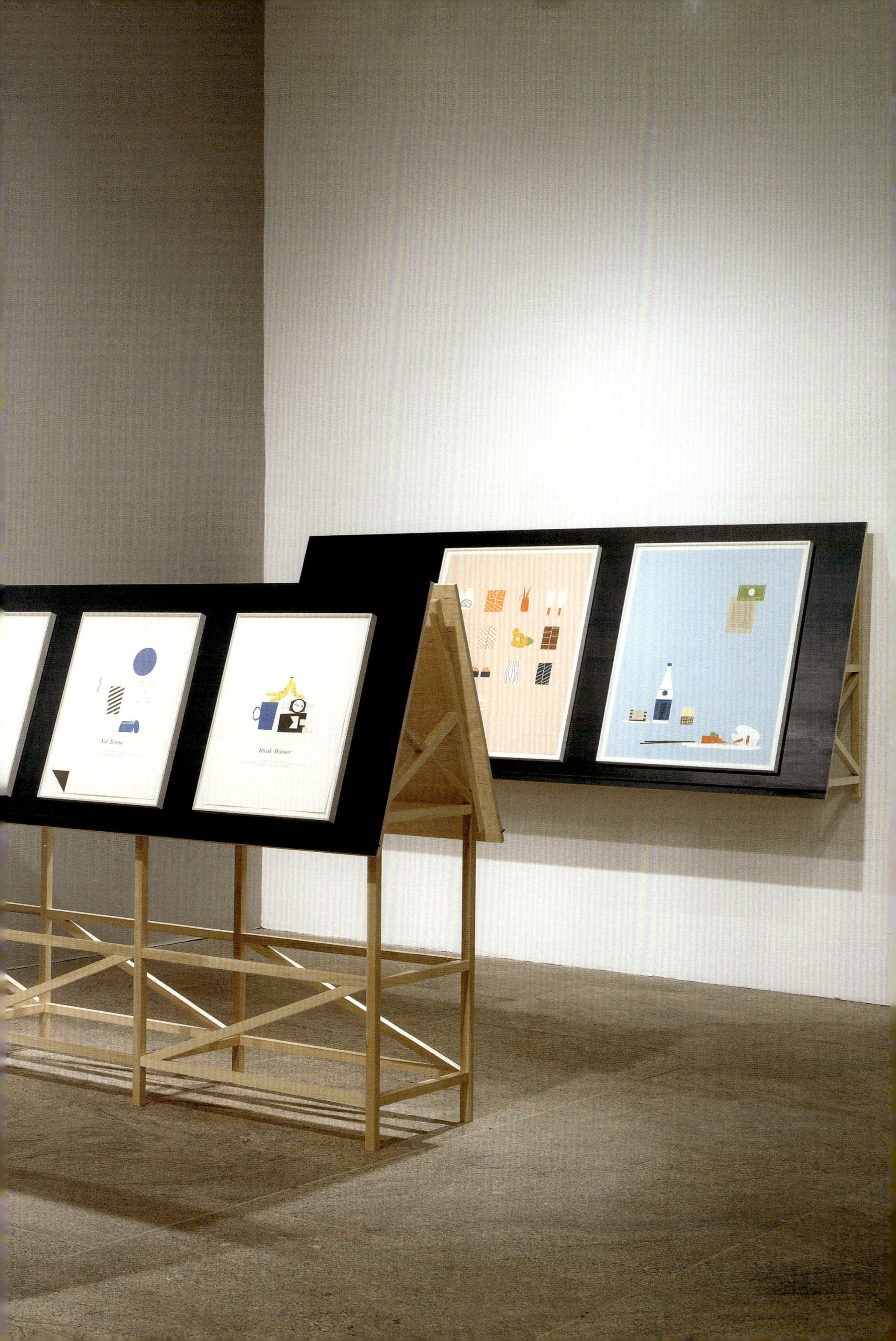
Not Young
Steak Dinner

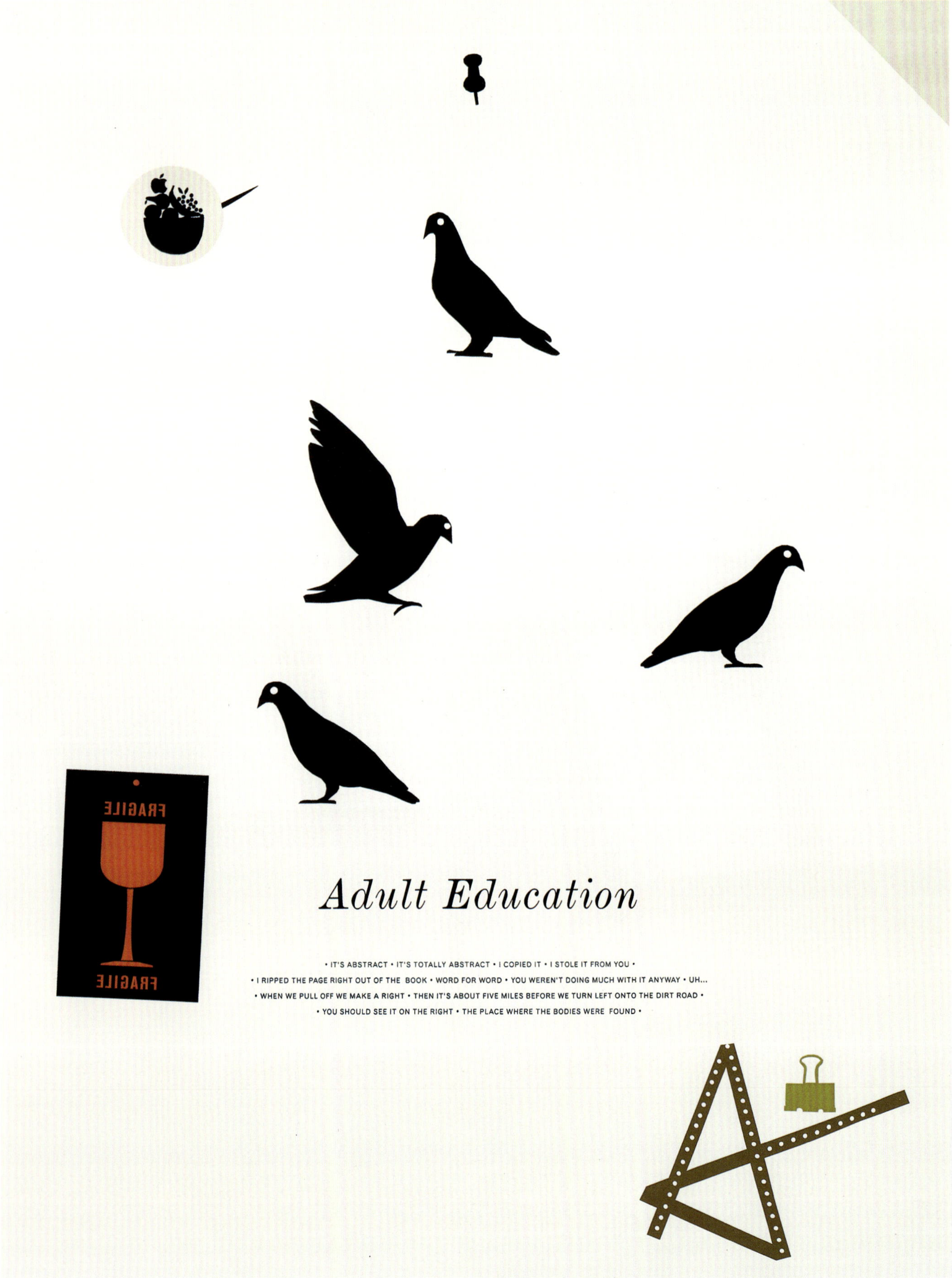
FRAGILE
FRAGILE
Adult Education
• IT'S ABSTRACT • IT'S TOTALLY ABSTRACT • I COPIED IT • I STOLE IT FROM YOU •
• I RIPPED THE PAGE RIGHT OUT OF THE BOOK • WORD FOR WORD • YOU WEREN'T DOING MUCH WITH IT ANYWAY • UH...
• WHEN WE PULL OFF WE MAKE A RIGHT • THEN IT'S ABOUT FIVE MILES BEFORE WE TURN LEFT ONTO THE DIRT ROAD •
• YOU SHOULD SEE IT ON THE RIGHT • THE PLACE WHERE THE BODIES WERE FOUND •

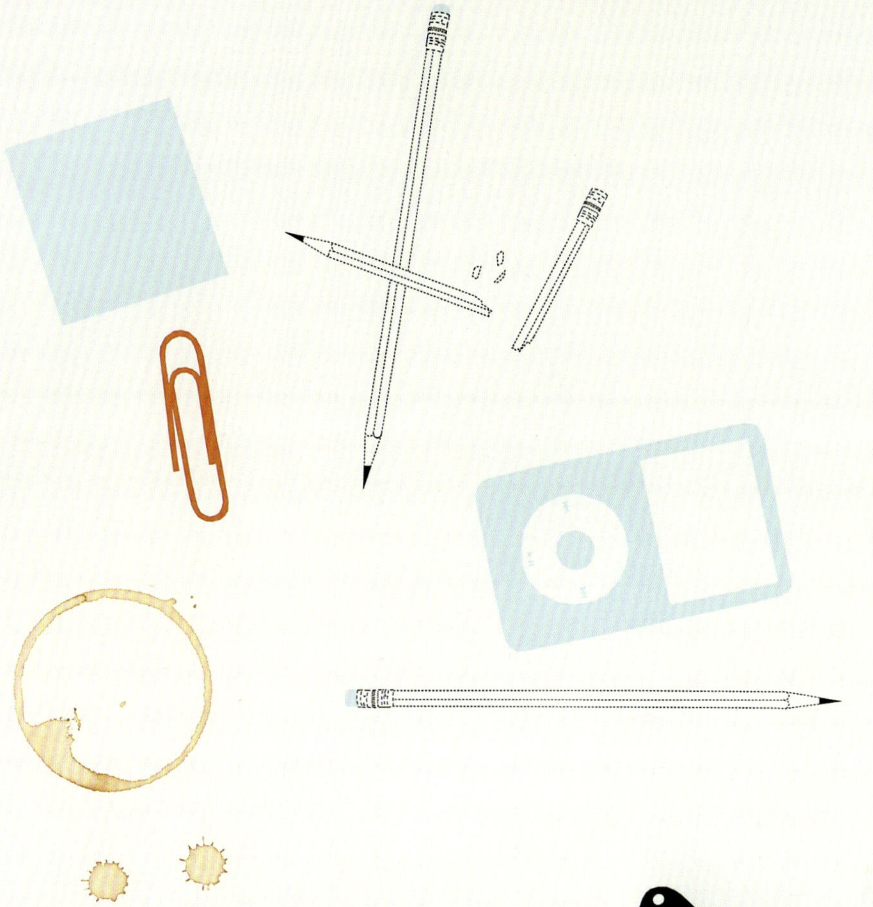

Pigs, Like Us

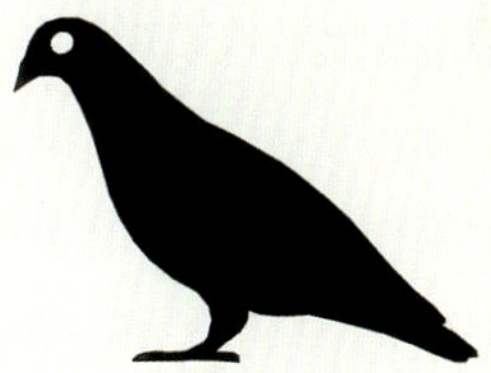

• THEY HAD TO PUMP HER STOMACH • AMAZING WHAT THEY FOUND •
• AMONG THE ARUGULA, WATERCRESS, BLUE-FIN TUNA, AGE-DRIED STEAK • THERE IT IS • YOUR HEART • AND LOOK... A BUNCH OF RAZOR BLADES •
• LITTLE LIGHT BULBS • COCAINE • LITTLE TRAVEL BOTTLES • ANTI-DEPRESSANTS • YOUR OLD UNTOUCHED JOB APPLICATION •

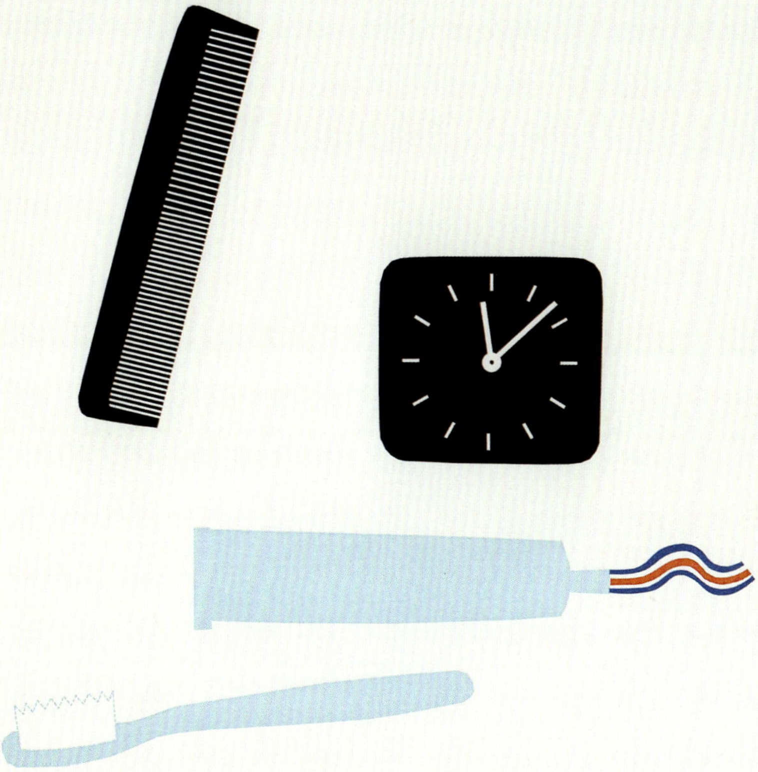

Pulling Out

• A BIT AGGRESSIVE? • WOULDN'T YOU SAY? • DIDN'T SEE THAT COMING •
• THE WAY HE SEEMED PREPARED TO ARGUE AT EVERY TURN • AND WHERE DID HE EVER GET THAT ABOUT YOU KNOW WHAT •
• SO ANGRY • SOMEWHAT LOST I FEAR • WORRIES ME THOUGH • IT'S AS IF HE'S DETERMINED TO DRAG US DOWN WITH HIM •

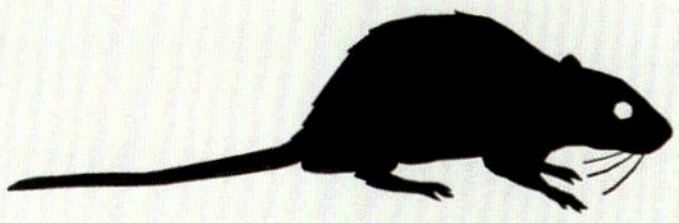

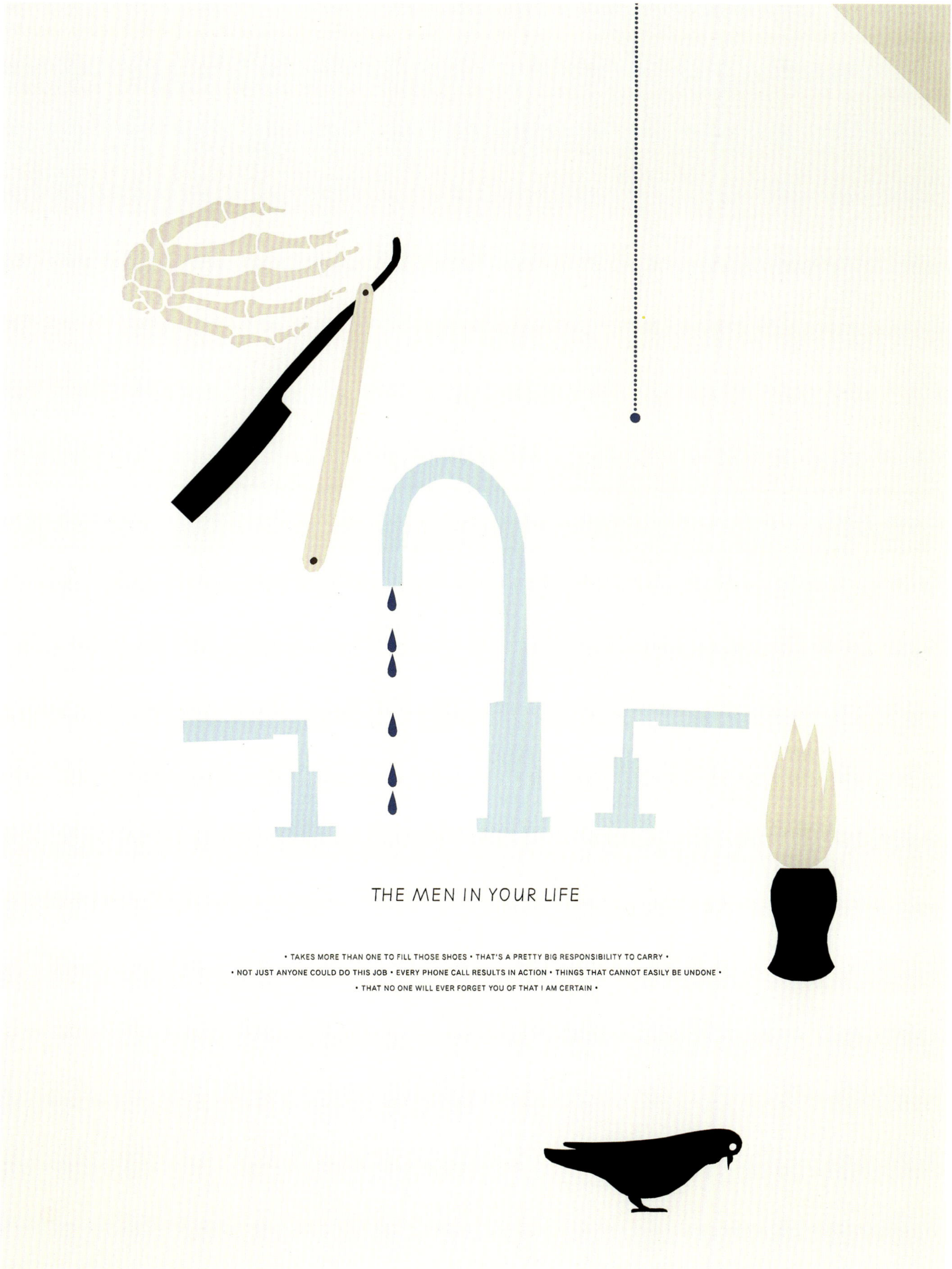
THE MEN IN YOUR LIFE
• TAKES MORE THAN ONE TO FILL THOSE SHOES • THAT'S A PRETTY BIG RESPONSIBILITY TO CARRY •
• NOT JUST ANYONE COULD DO THIS JOB • EVERY PHONE CALL RESULTS IN ACTION • THINGS THAT CANNOT EASILY BE UNDONE •
• THAT NO ONE WILL EVER FORGET YOU OF THAT I AM CERTAIN •

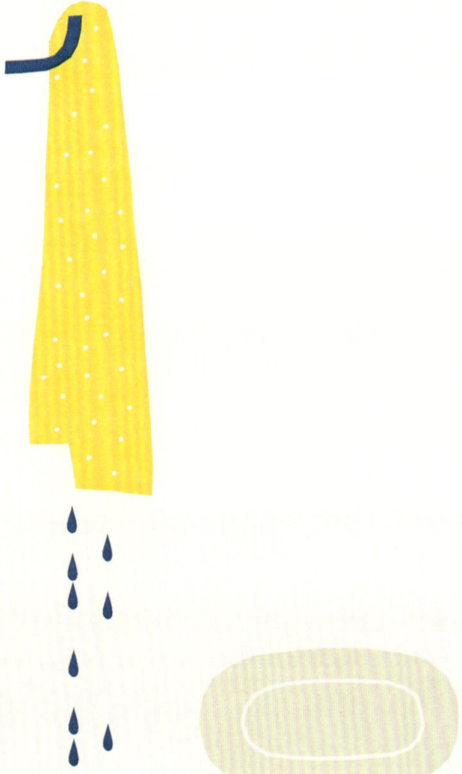

Alarm Clock

• WHEN HE WRITES HE SEES HIMSELF AS SOMEONE ELSE • AS SOMEONE WHO WRITES WELL •
• AND WHEN HE TALKS TO OTHERS ABOUT WHAT IT IS HE DOES • HE PICTURES SOMEONE ELSE • A CONVERSATIONALIST BEYOND COMPARE •
• AND WHEN HE'S HOME AT NIGHT TRYING TO SLEEP • HE SEES HIMSELF AS A GROSS PIG THAT EVERYONE HATES •

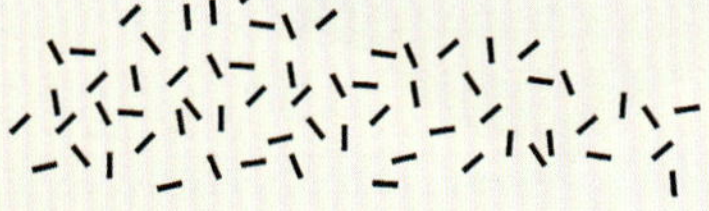

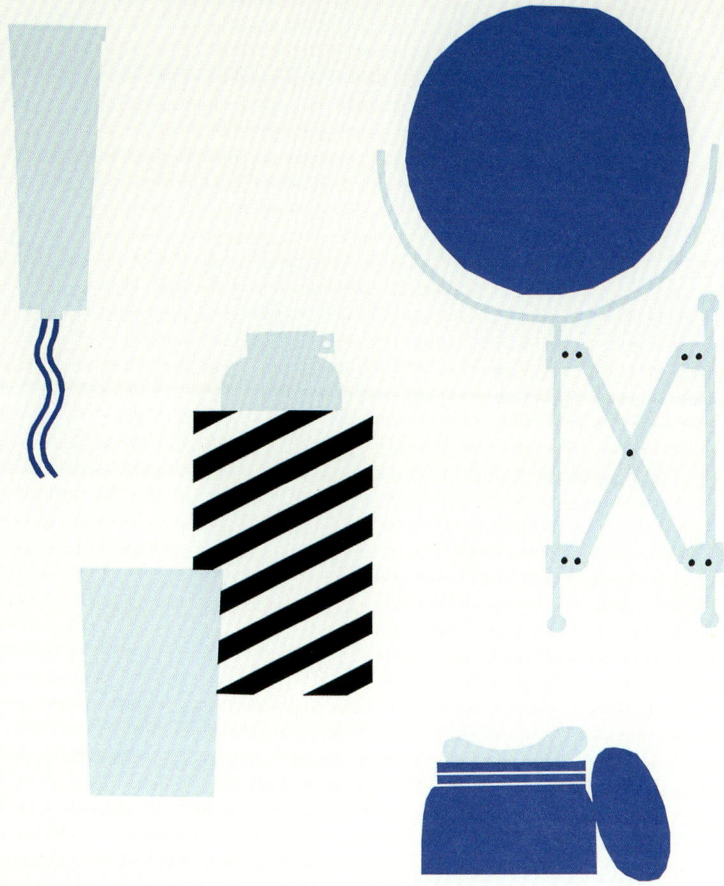

Not Young

• STEPPING ON A SNAKE'S HEAD • ITS TAIL WRAPPING AROUND YOUR LEG •
• SPITTING INTO A CAGE • SETTING FIRE TO A NEST • DRAGGING THE OCEAN FLOORS • SERVING THE LAST OF THE MEAT • CLEARING TABLES AND STORING FEARS •
• WATCHED IT HAPPEN • SAW THE SEX IN FRONT OF EVERYTHING •

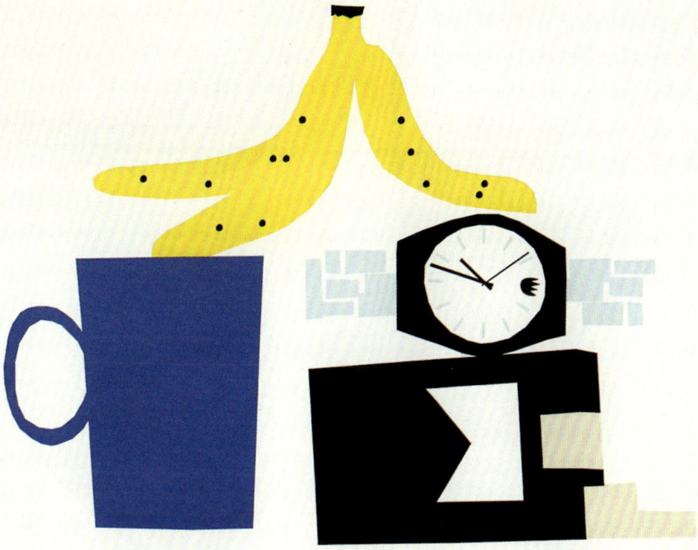

Steak Dinner

• THIS YEAR TELL HER YOU LOVE HER ALL OVER AGAIN •
• WITH A GRAB BAG OF DIAMONDS • WITH MOUTHFULS OF CAVIAR • WITH YOUR RENT IN CLOTHES • A CREDIT CARD OF HOTEL ROOMS •
• STOCKINGS • CHAMPAGNE • PLANE TICKETS • AND A SOFT SLAP ON HER BARE ASS •

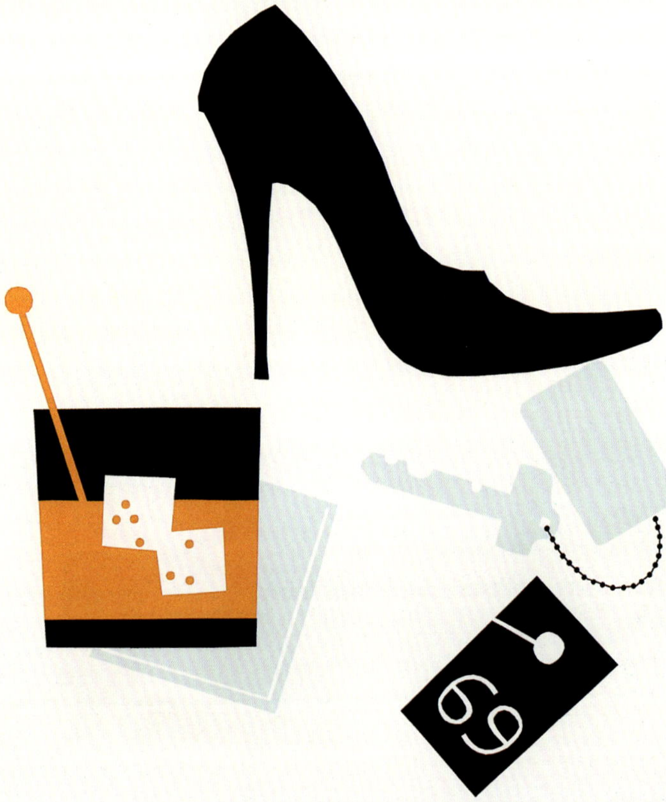

Raw Bar

• NO – IT WOULDN'T END SO QUICKLY • IT WAS GOING TO BE A MORE DRAWN OUT AFFAIR •
• I WAS GOING TO HAVE TO LIVE THOSE YEARS • I WAS GOING TO HAVE TO TAKE CARE OF MYSELF •
• THE NOVEL STARTS WITH THIS IDEA OF AN END • A FILM BEGINS WITH ANOTHER'S CREDITS •

• WANTED TO TALK ABOUT AN ABUSIVE LIFESTYLE • WANTED TO ADDRESS HOW IT ALL GOES WRONG •

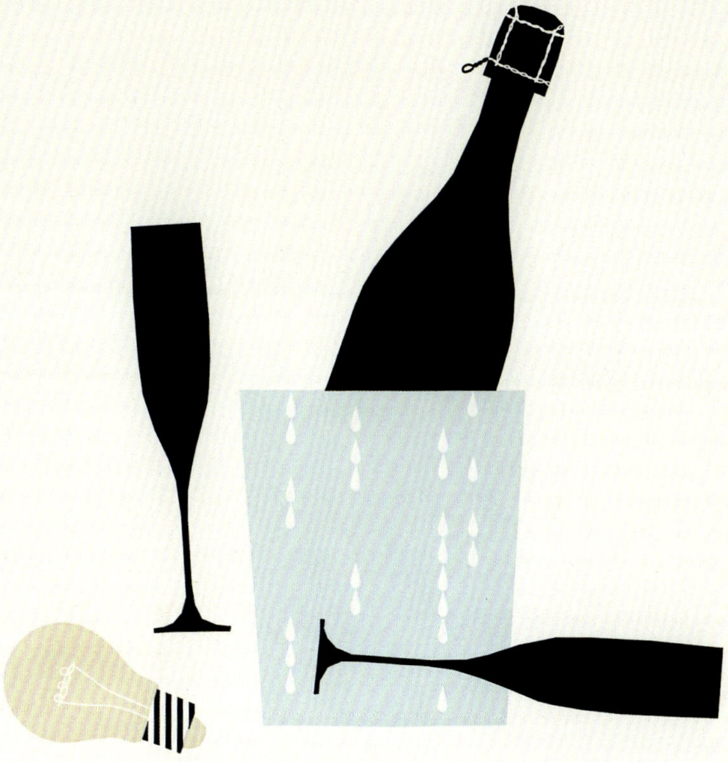

Ladies Choice

• IT LOOKS RIGHT • BUT IT ISN'T •

• JUST LOOKS LIKE SOMETHING YOU ALREADY THINK YOU LIKE • BUT MAYBE • JUST MAYBE • YOU DON'T LIKE IT AT ALL •

• I COULD BE WRONG •

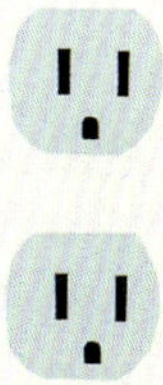

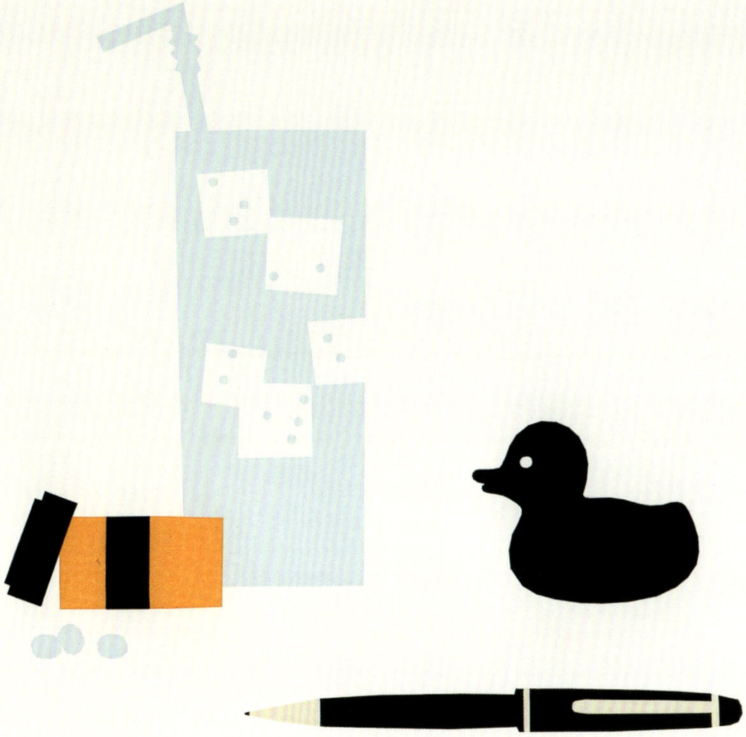

Intellectual Condom

• I KNOW YOU KNOW I KNOW •
• YOU KNOW I KNOW YOU KNOW I KNOW •
• YOU KNOW I KNOW I KNOW YOU KNOW •
• I KNOW YOU DIDN'T DO IT •

• BUT THAT'S NOT WHAT MATTERS NOW •

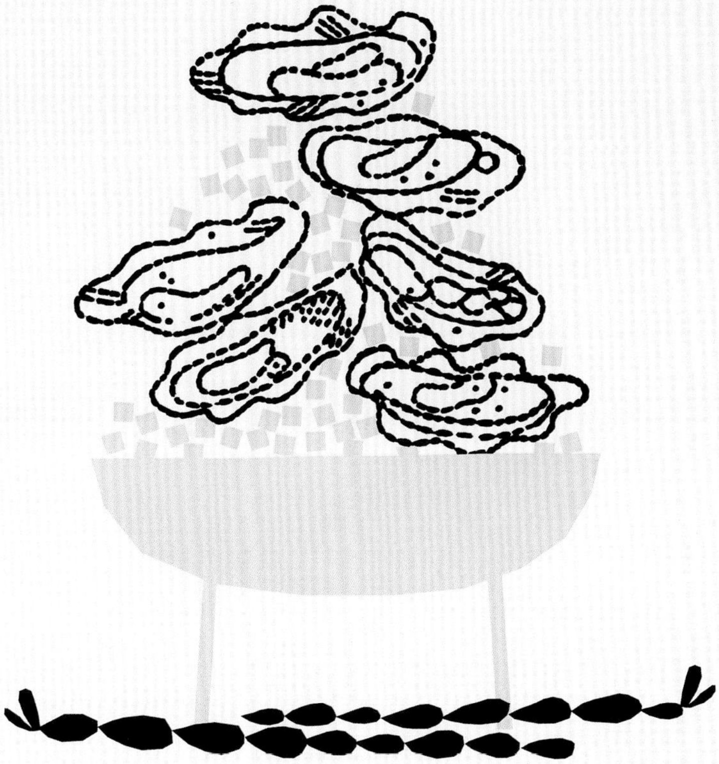

Say It Again

• WHEN YOU READ THIS I WILL BE DEAD •
• WELL IF NOT REALLY DEAD - THEN ONE DAY • AND YOU TOO - ONE DAY • WILL BE DEAD • BUT EVEN THEN • ONE COULD SAY •
• THAT YOU HAD READ THIS •

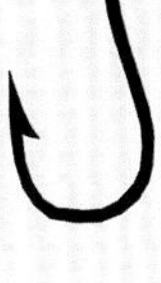

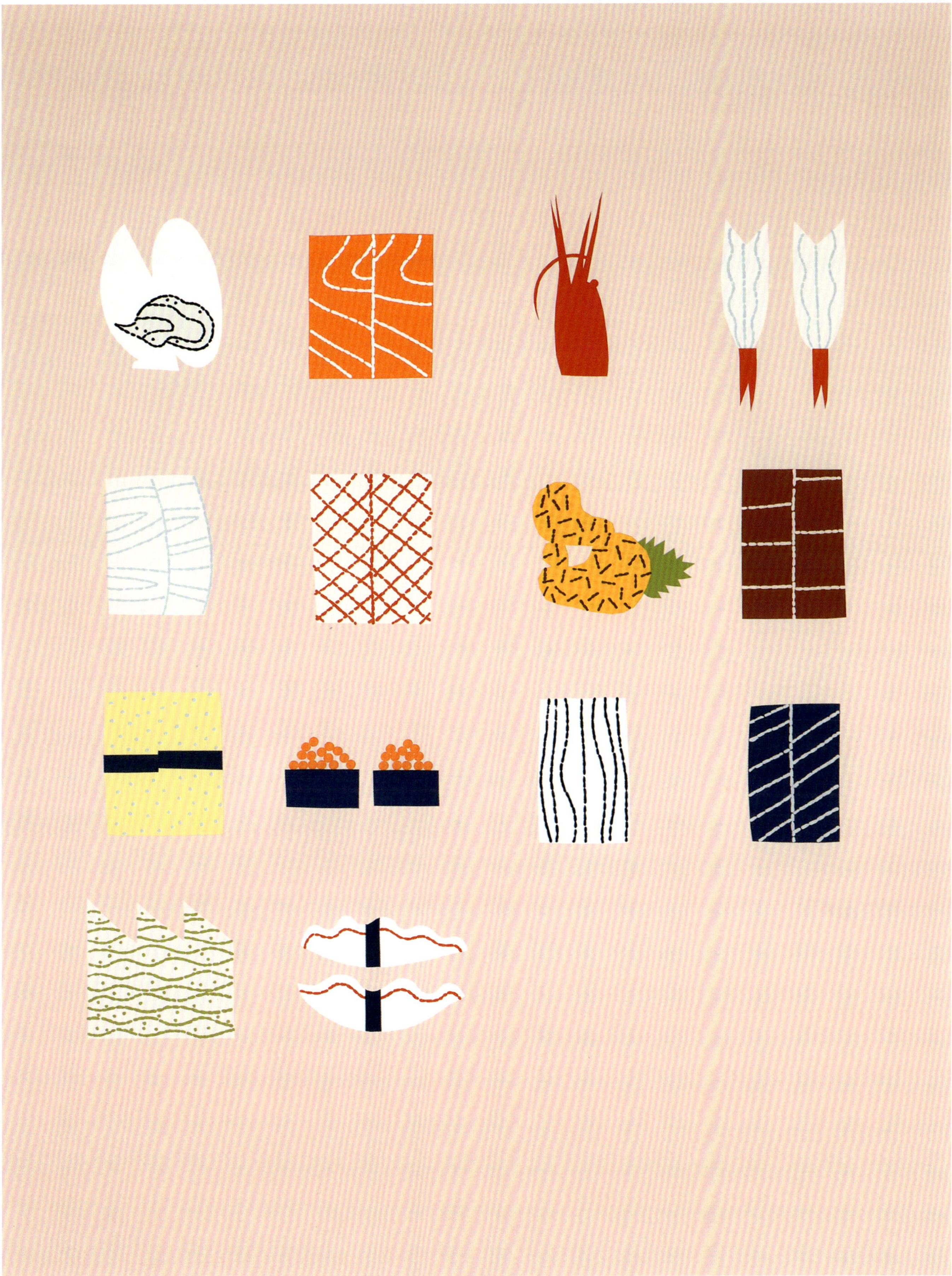

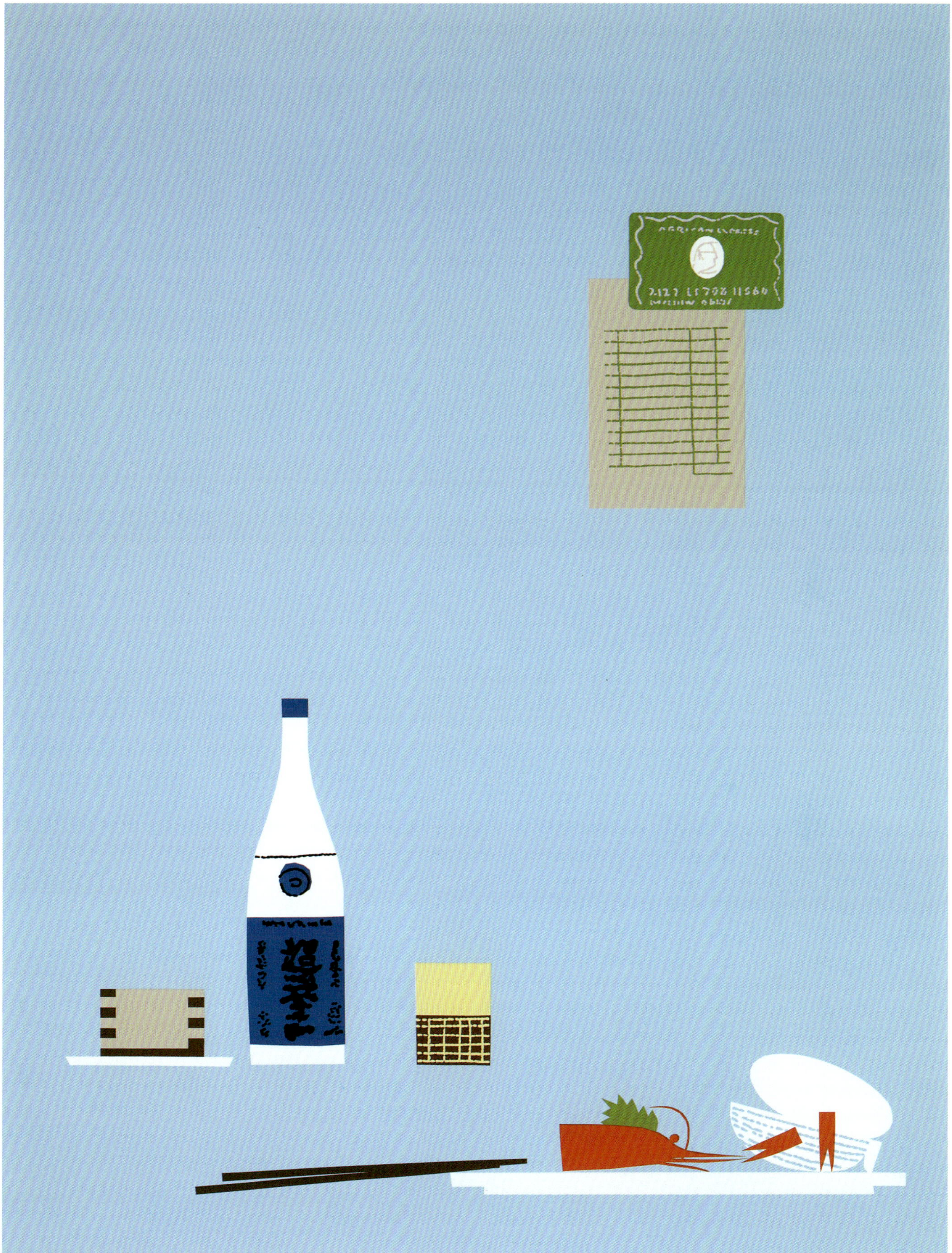

JFK International Airport

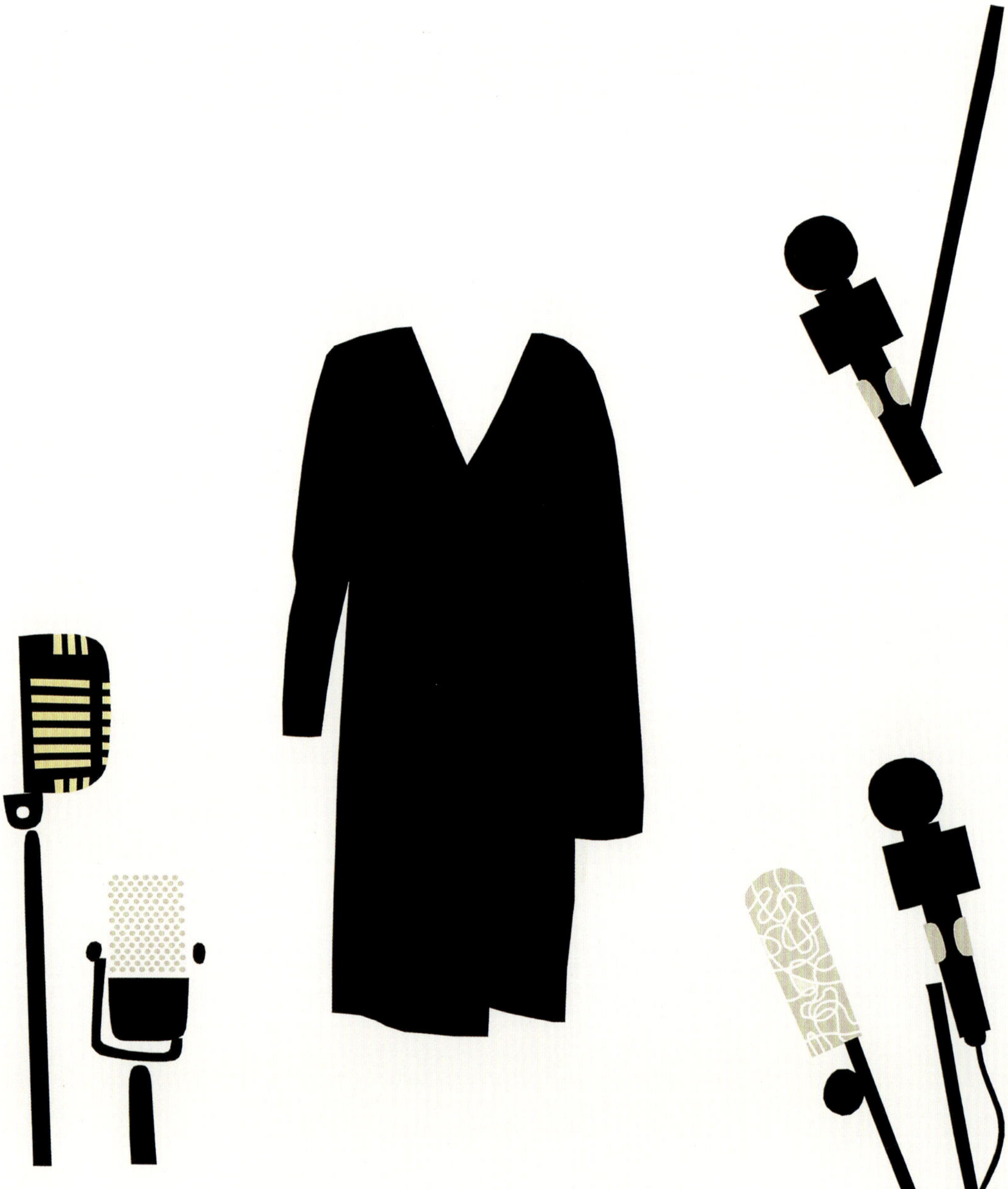

BIRTHDAY CAKE

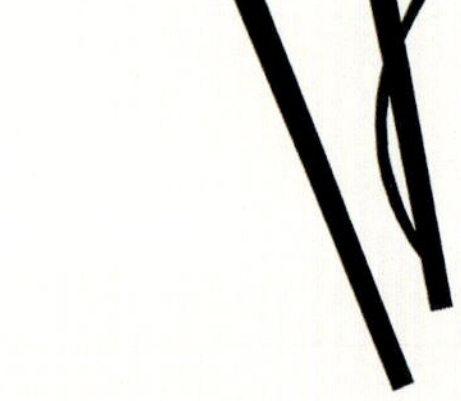

• NOT THE ADVICE I WOULD HAVE GIVEN • BUT - OK, SO SHE KNOWS • IT'S NOT LIKE IT WAS THAT EXPENSIVE •
• HAS THE TEXTURE OF ... • THE TASTE OF SEAFOOD • REMINDS ME OF SOMETHING I TRIED TO FORGET •

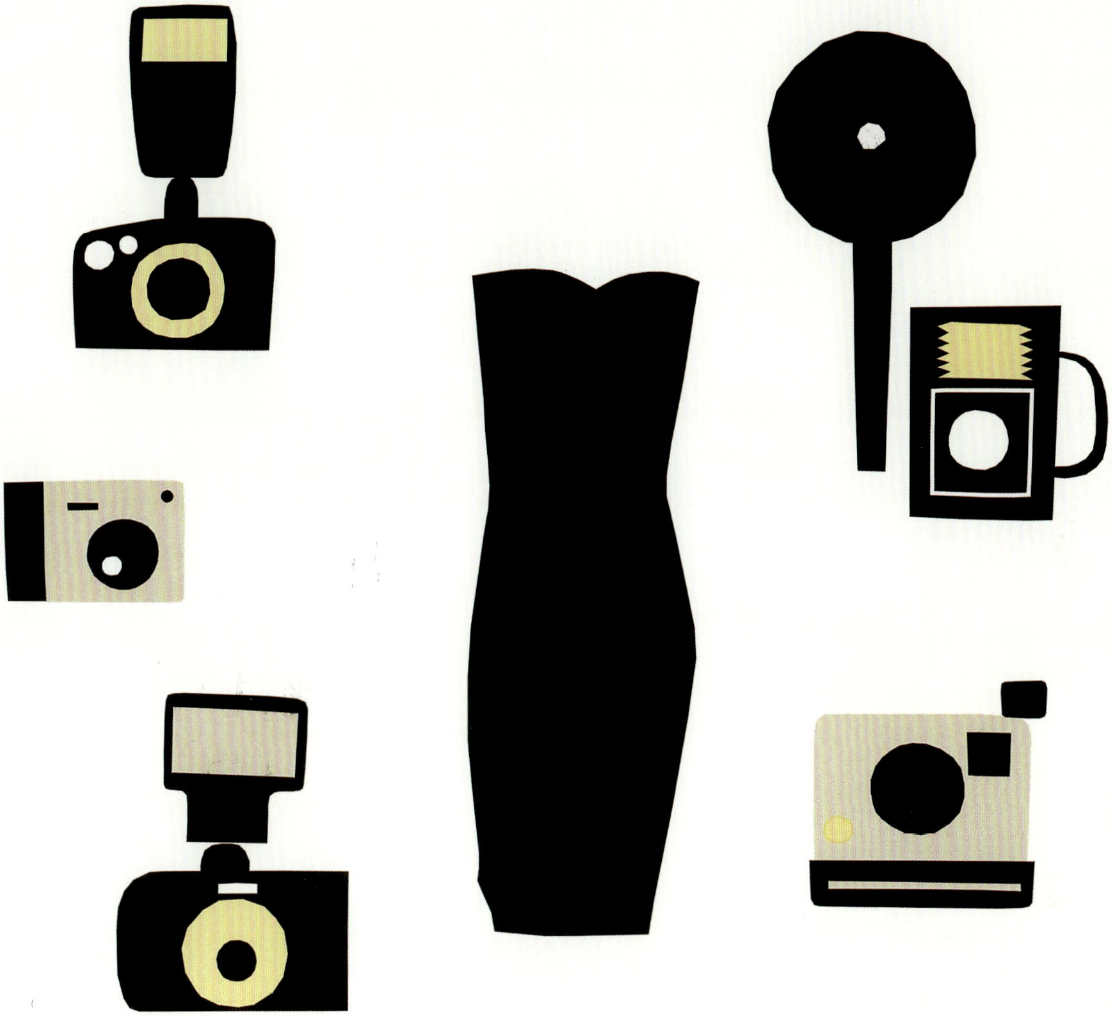

DRINKING GAMES

• STEPPING IN SHIT IN PARIS • SLEEPING IN IN TOKYO • BREAKING A FEVER IN BERLIN •
• CLEANING POOLS IN LOS ANGELES • LOSING HAIR IN LONDON • PAYING FOR IT IN NEW YORK •
• YOU HAVE TO REPEAT WHAT IT WAS YOU ASKED FOR • SPIT IT OUT BEFORE ANYONE SEES •

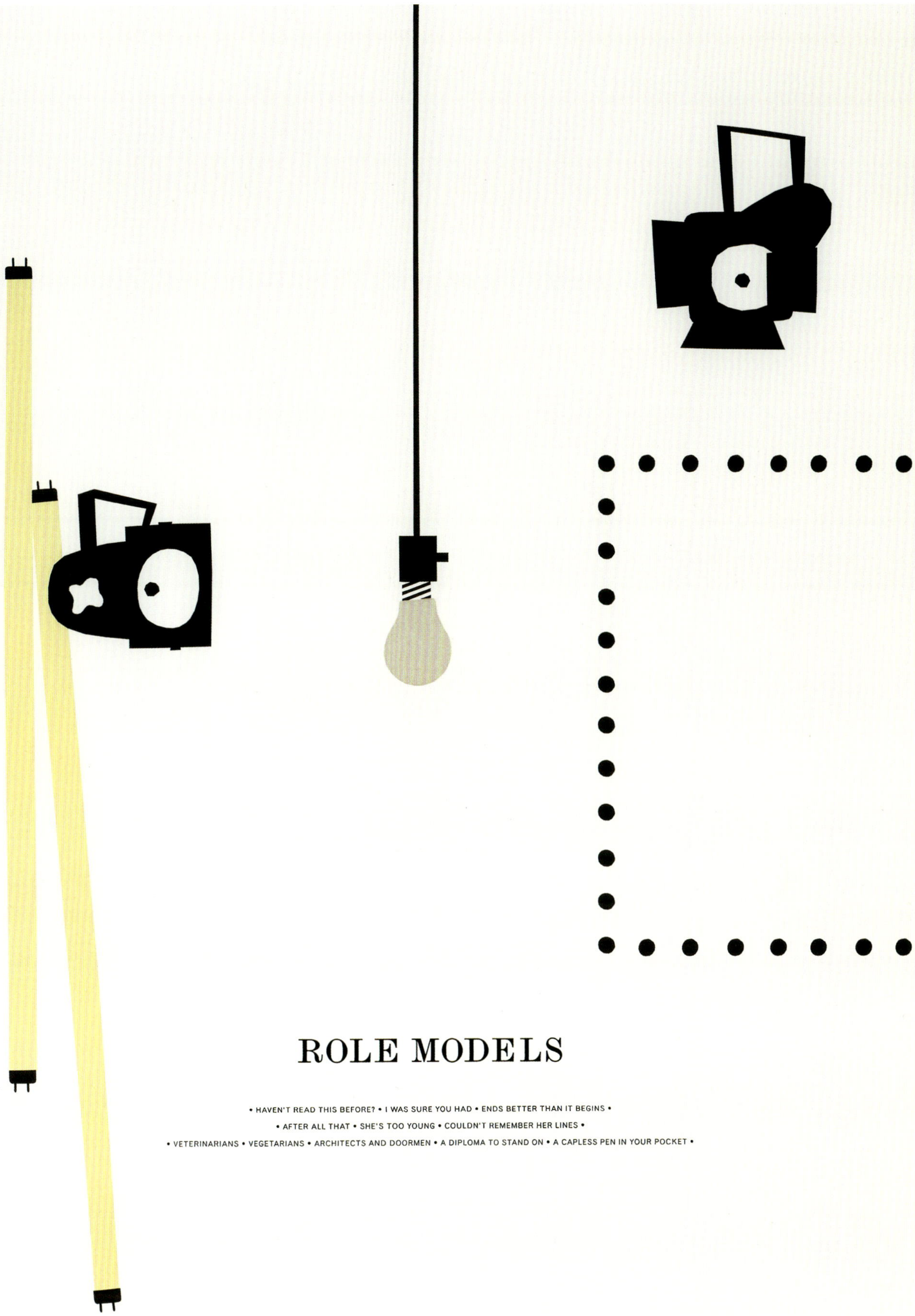

ROLE MODELS

• HAVEN'T READ THIS BEFORE? • I WAS SURE YOU HAD • ENDS BETTER THAN IT BEGINS •
• AFTER ALL THAT • SHE'S TOO YOUNG • COULDN'T REMEMBER HER LINES •
• VETERINARIANS • VEGETARIANS • ARCHITECTS AND DOORMEN • A DIPLOMA TO STAND ON • A CAPLESS PEN IN YOUR POCKET •

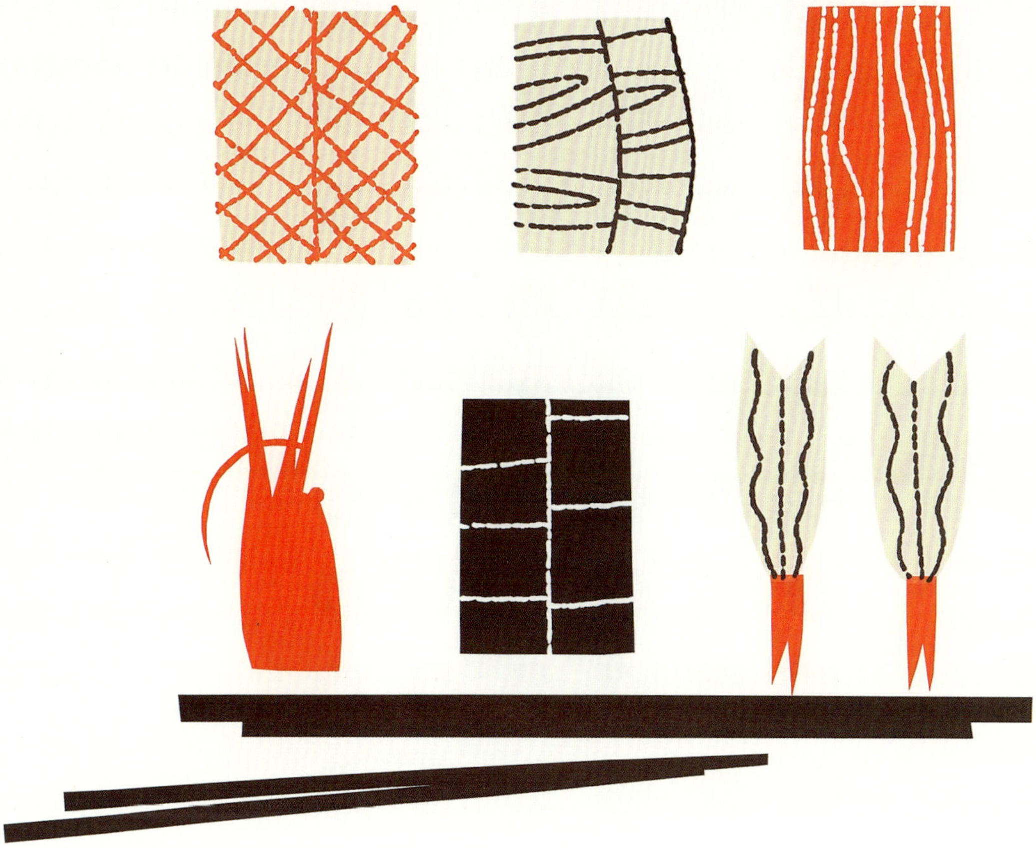

A WELL PISSED ON TREE

· I DIDN'T SAY THAT · SOMEONE ELSE DID · I'M NOT DRUNK ·
· I MEAN EVEN IF I AM I CAN STILL THINK CLEARLY · PERHAPS CLEARER THAN IF I WAS SOBER ·
· I FEEL LIKE A BAD PERSON ALL THE TIME · SOMETIMES THERE ARE HINTS OF WHAT I'VE DONE RIGHT ·
· BUT REALLY I'M ACTIVELY, CONSTANTLY, AND FURIOUSLY LOOKING FOR SIGNS THAT I'VE DONE SOMETHING WRONG ·
· SHE REMINDS ME CONSTANTLY OF WHAT A LOSER I AM ·

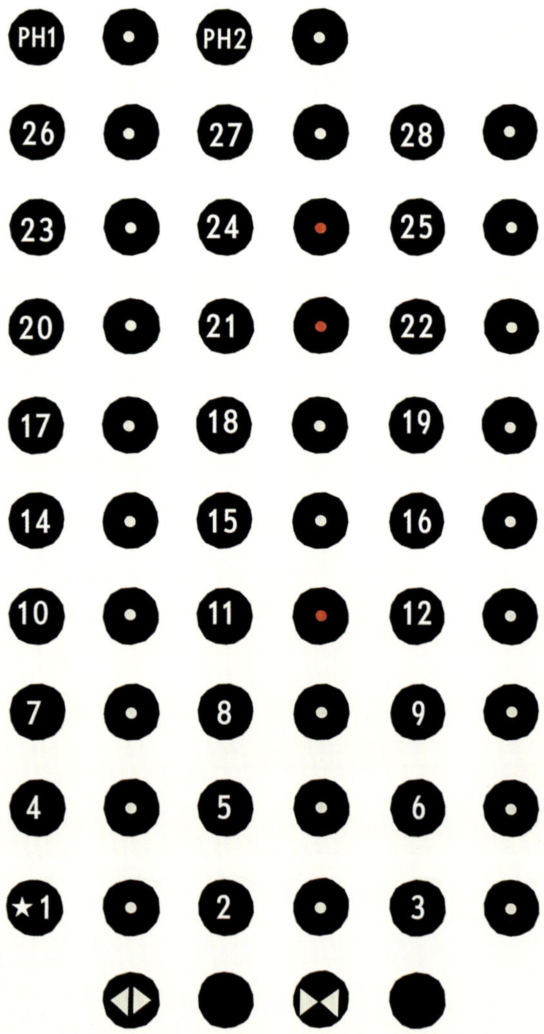

BUT YOU DO IT ANYWAY

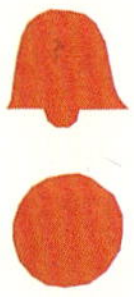

· UP TWENTY-FOUR FLOORS · ALL THE WAY IN THE BACK · IN THE SUITE · IN THE BATHROOM ·
· A COUNTER OF COSMETICS · LIPSTICK IN THE SINK · SMASHED GLASS AND TOWELS ON THE FLOOR ·
· PINK LIGHT FROM ABOVE THE MIRRORS · A SHOWER CURTAIN HALF TORN OFF ITS RINGS · WALLPAPER PATTERNED MINT AND BRONZE ·
· THE HUM OF THE AIR CONDITIONING · THE DRIPS IN THE TUB · AN UNANSWERED PHONE RINGING IN THE DARK ·

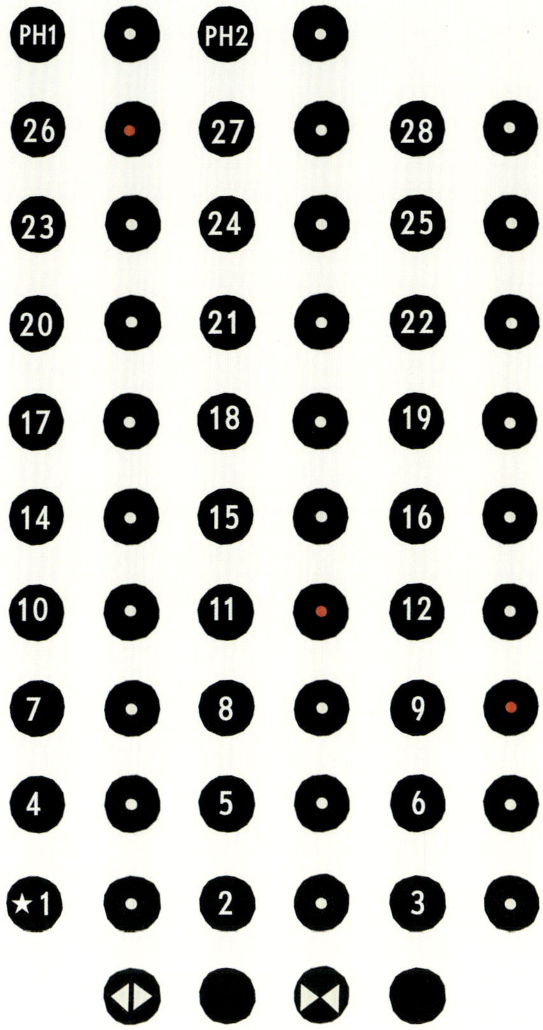

YOUR LAST NAME FIRST

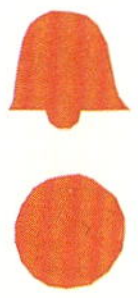

· AT LAST I UNDERSTOOD WHAT HE WAS TRYING TO SAY ·
· HE WASN'T BEING MEAN AND HE WASN'T ANGRY · HE DIDN'T KNOW A THING · HE HADN'T BEEN BACK TO THE HOTEL ·
· I WAS GOING TO HAVE TO GO TO AFRICA ALONE · I WAS GOING TO HAVE TO BEAR THE HEATED NIGHTS, THE INSECTS, THE CROWDED AIRPORTS ·
· I MIGHT EVEN GET AWAY WITH IT · I WOULD AVOID THE SHAME · BUT I WOULD NEVER SEE YOU AGAIN ·

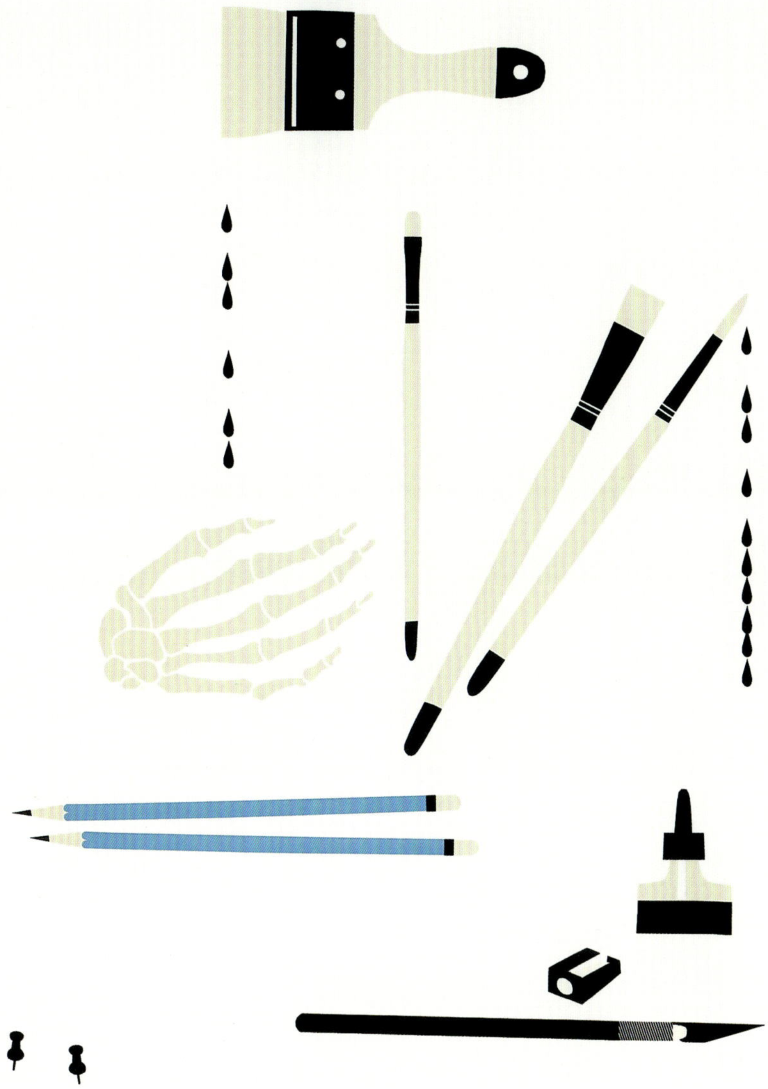

Decide Against

• WASN'T WHAT WE HOPED FOR • OUR EXPECTATIONS • OUR FEARS • BOTH INAPPROPRIATE AND EXTREME •
• DIDN'T HIT THE BRAKES FAST ENOUGH • WOKE TO THE SOUND OF GUNS LOADING • TEETH BEING BRUSHED • THE SCRAPE OF THE RAZOR •
• AGAIN DIET • AGAIN DEBT • AGAIN WAR •

• AT THE SIDE OF THE STAGE • IN THE DARK • LOOKING OUT • PAST THE GLARING LIGHTS • INTO THE BORED FACES AND PLUSH CHAIRS •
• IN THE BACK ROW • IN HAND • AN UNLIT CIGARETTE • CLICKING HIS FINGERNAILS WITH THE OTHER • HE CAN READ BETWEEN THE LINES •

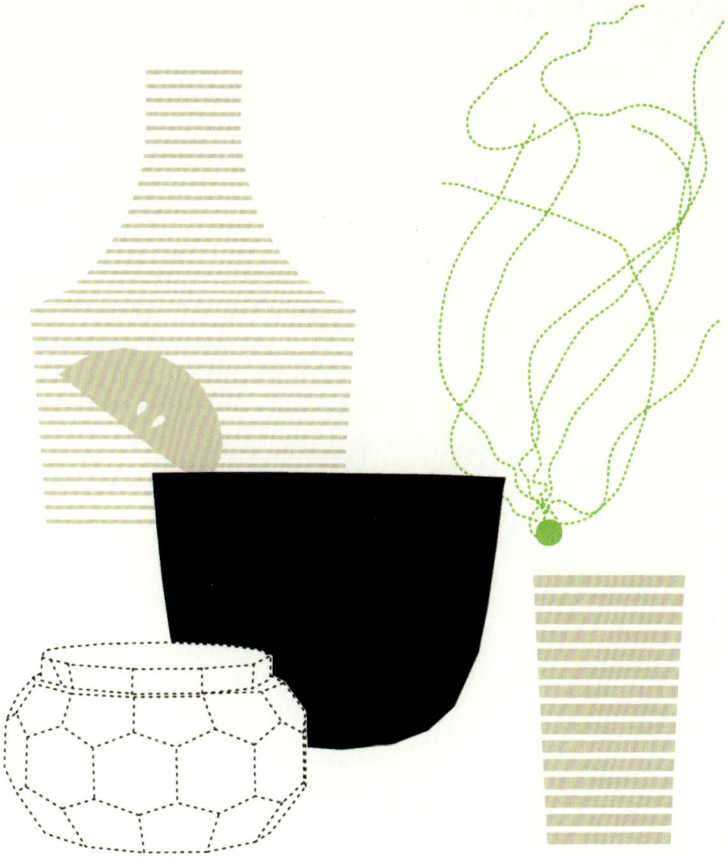

Teachers Fuck Students

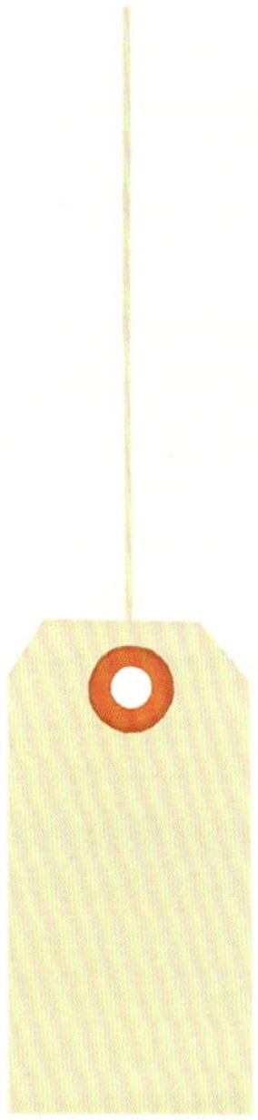

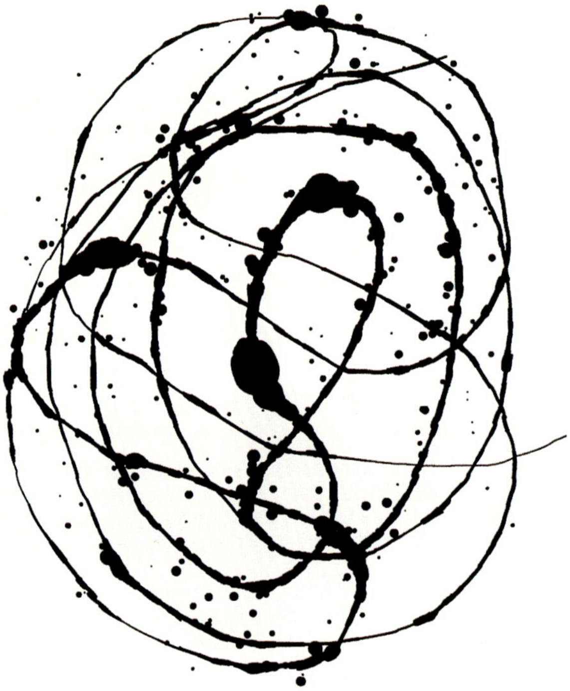

BLOW HARD

YES · OH GOD · YES · YES · FUCK YES · THAT'S IT · THAT'S IT · YES · OH GOD · JESUS CHRIST
YES · YES · OH GOD · NO · NO · OH NO · THAT'S IT · YES · YES · FUCK YES

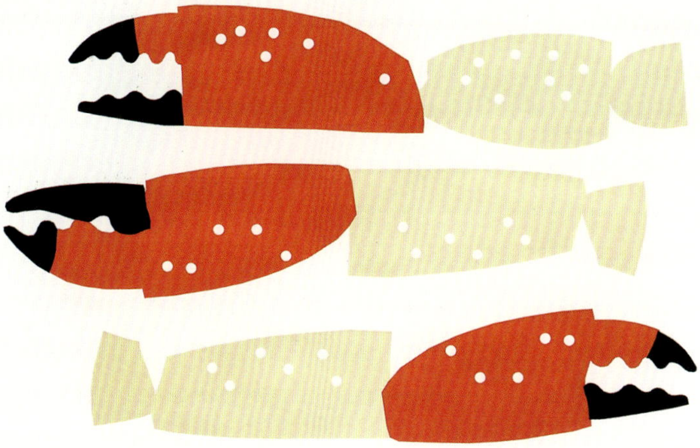

BLANK CHECK

THAT'S NOT WHAT I'M SAYING · YOU'VE GOT IT ALL WRONG · IT HAS NOTHING TO DO WITH ...
I DON'T KNOW THE FIRST THING ABOUT ... I'VE NEVER EVEN BEEN TO ... NOW PULL YOURSELF TOGETHER
YOU KNOW I WOULDN'T ASK IF IT WASN'T IMPORTANT · IT'S NOTHING YOU HAVEN'T DONE BEFORE

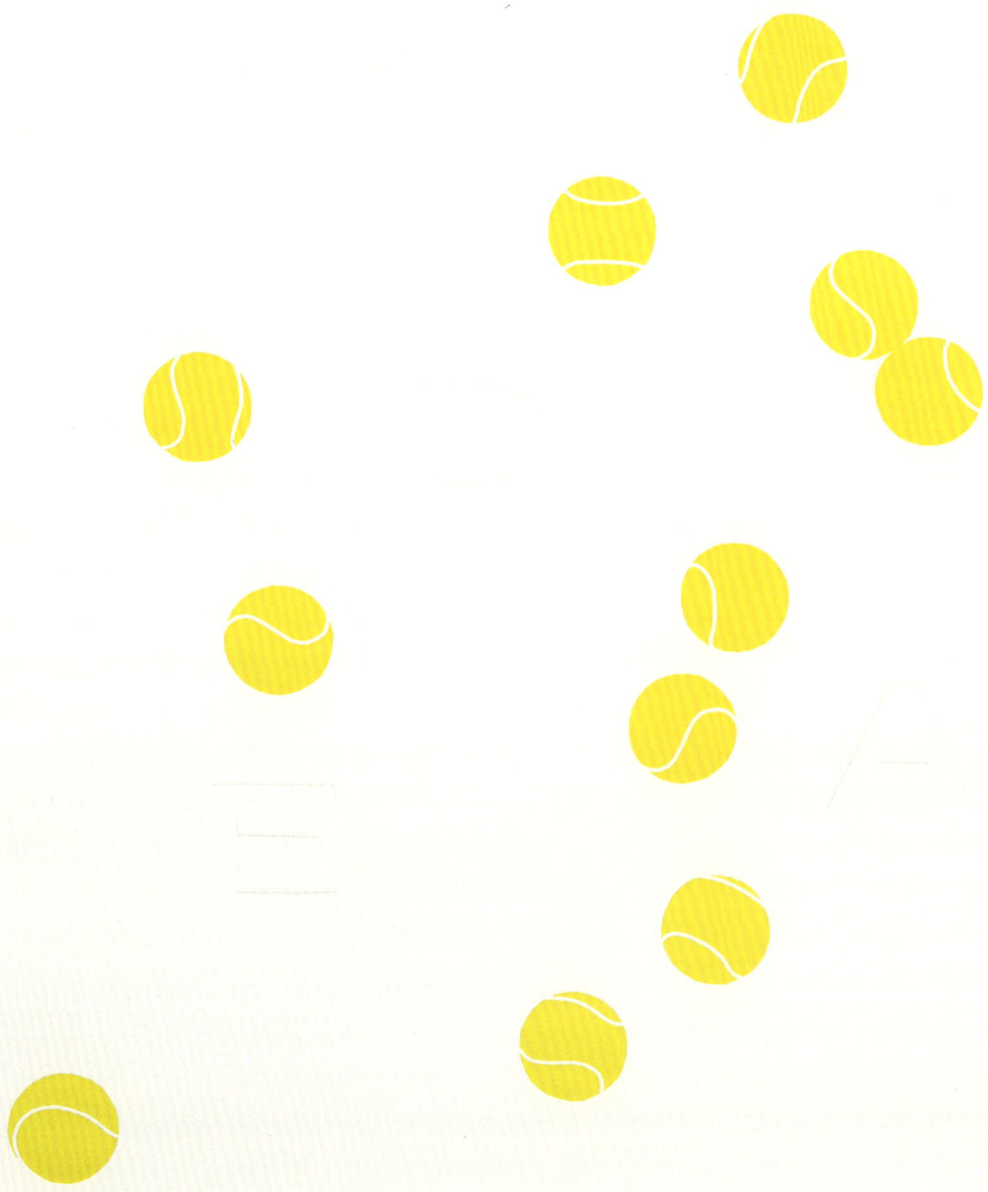

NEW MONEY

STOP CRYING · IT ISN'T HELPING · YOU DIDN'T DO THIS · YOU HAVE NOTHING TO DO WITH THIS
YOU SHOULDN'T EVEN BE HERE · JUST WASH YOUR FACE AND GO BACK TO THE HOTEL · AND DON'T SAY ANYTHING
YOU DIDN'T SEE ANYTHING · YOU DIDN'T HEAR ANYTHING · ALL YOU'VE DONE IS WATCH T.V. AND DRINK

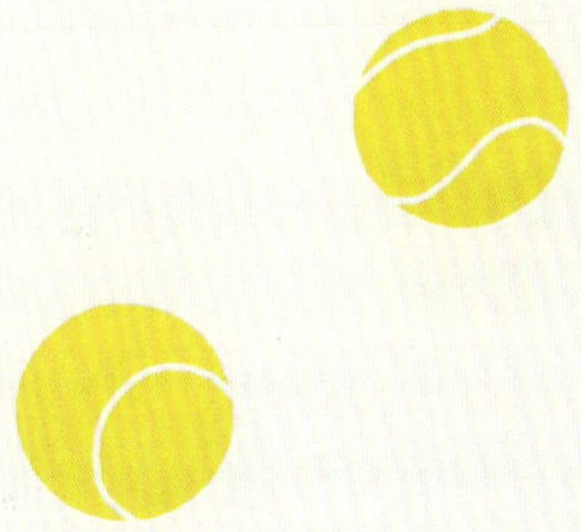

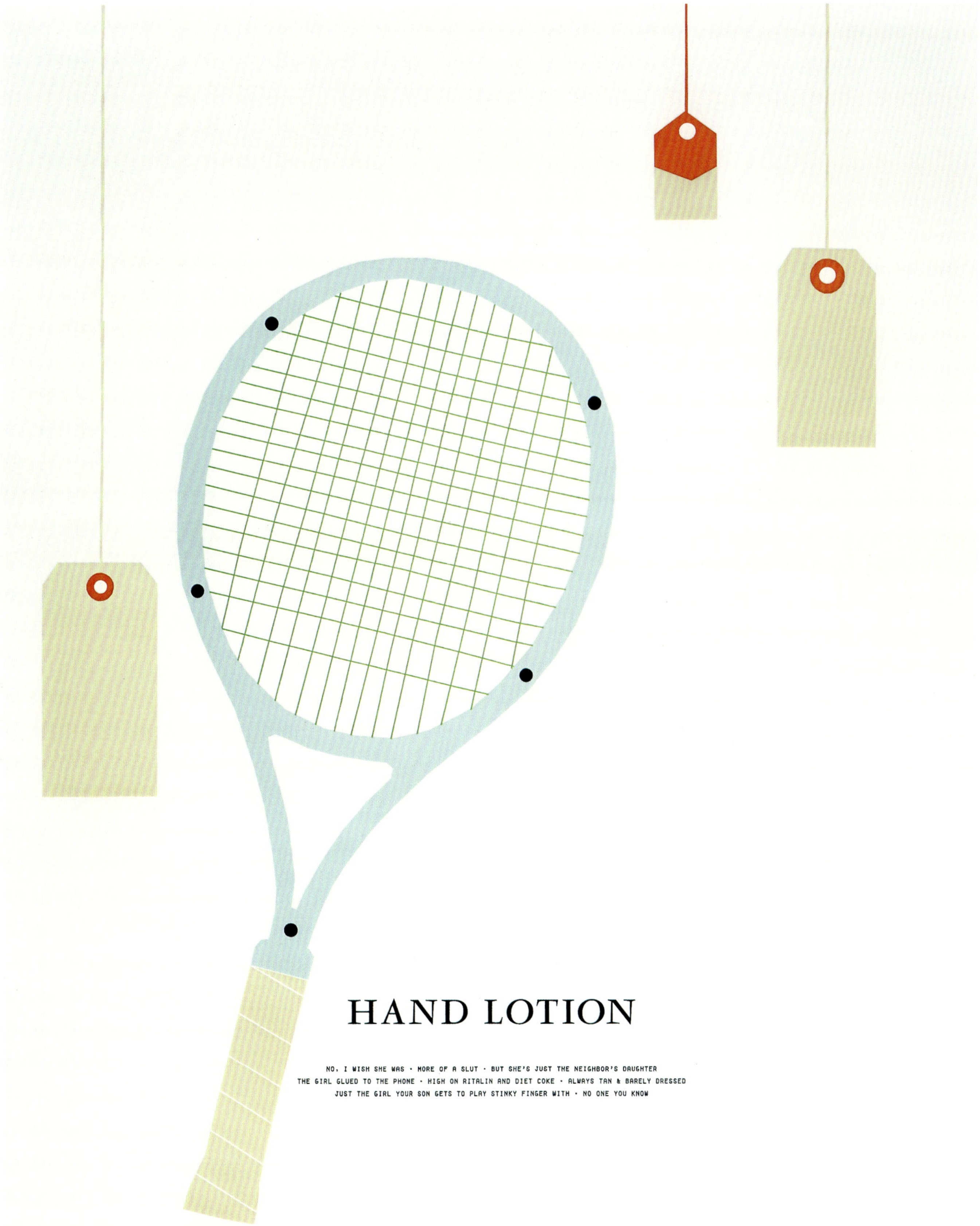

HAND LOTION

NO, I WISH SHE WAS · MORE OF A SLUT · BUT SHE'S JUST THE NEIGHBOR'S DAUGHTER
THE GIRL GLUED TO THE PHONE · HIGH ON RITALIN AND DIET COKE · ALWAYS TAN & BARELY DRESSED
JUST THE GIRL YOUR SON GETS TO PLAY STINKY FINGER WITH · NO ONE YOU KNOW

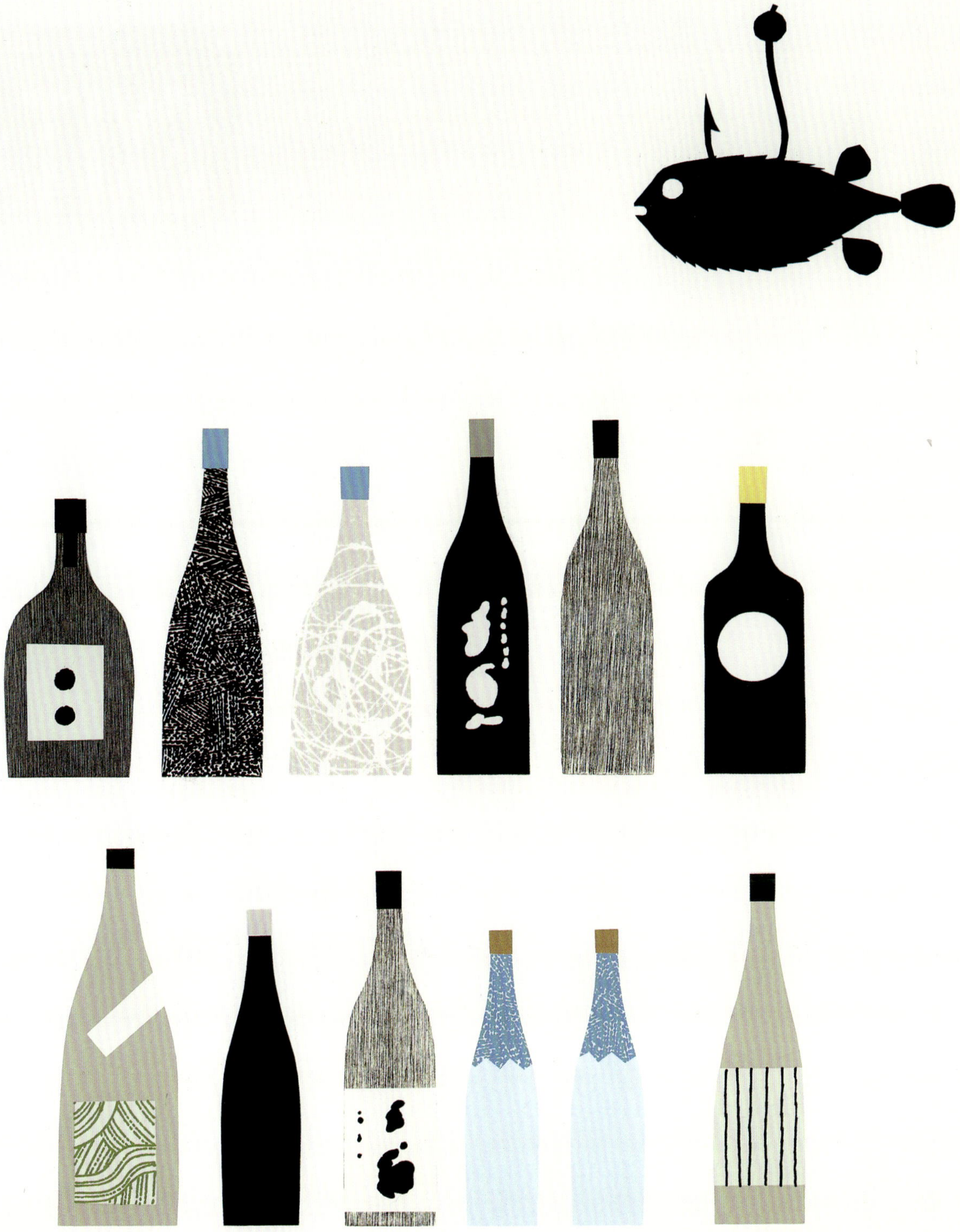

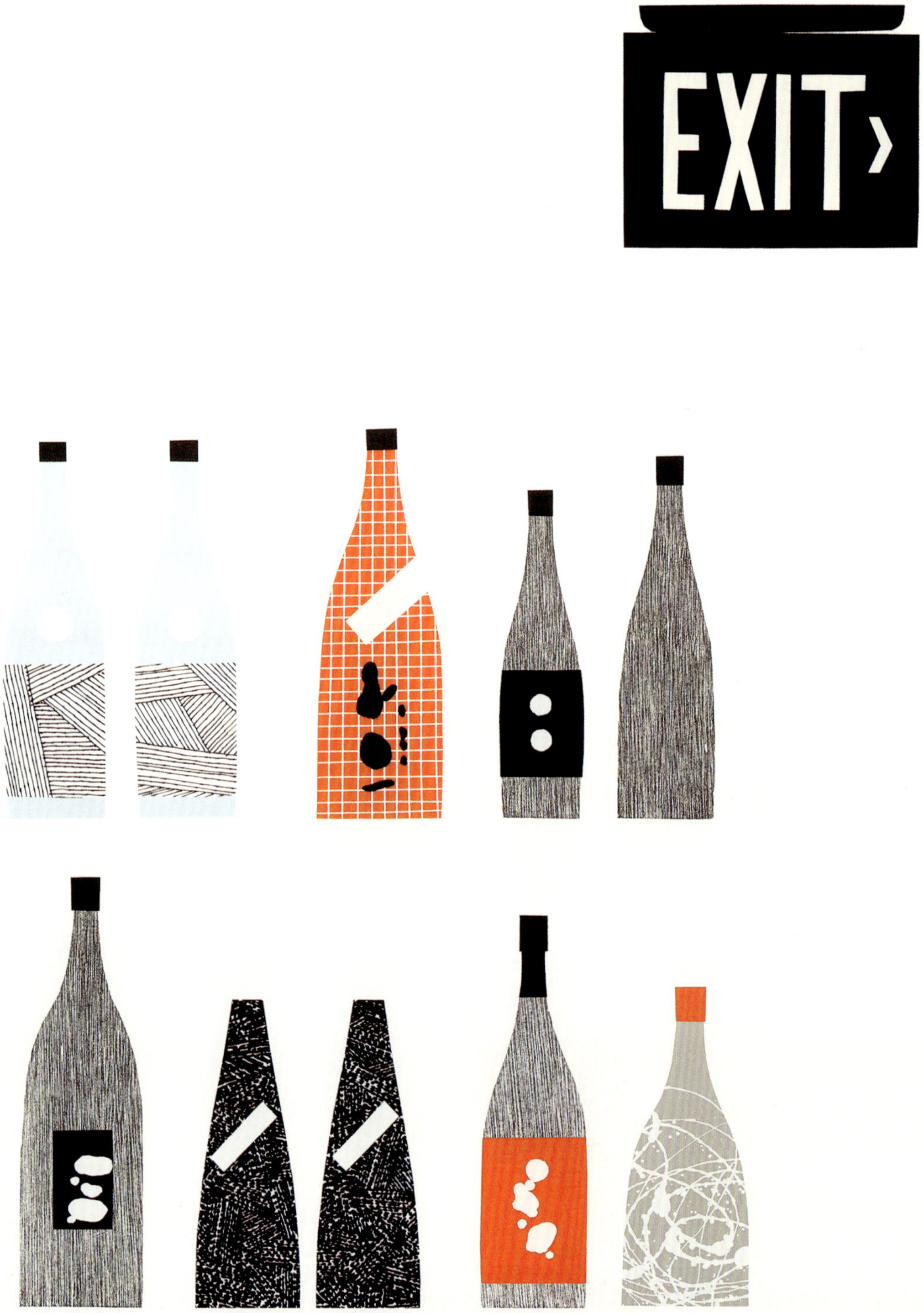
EXIT

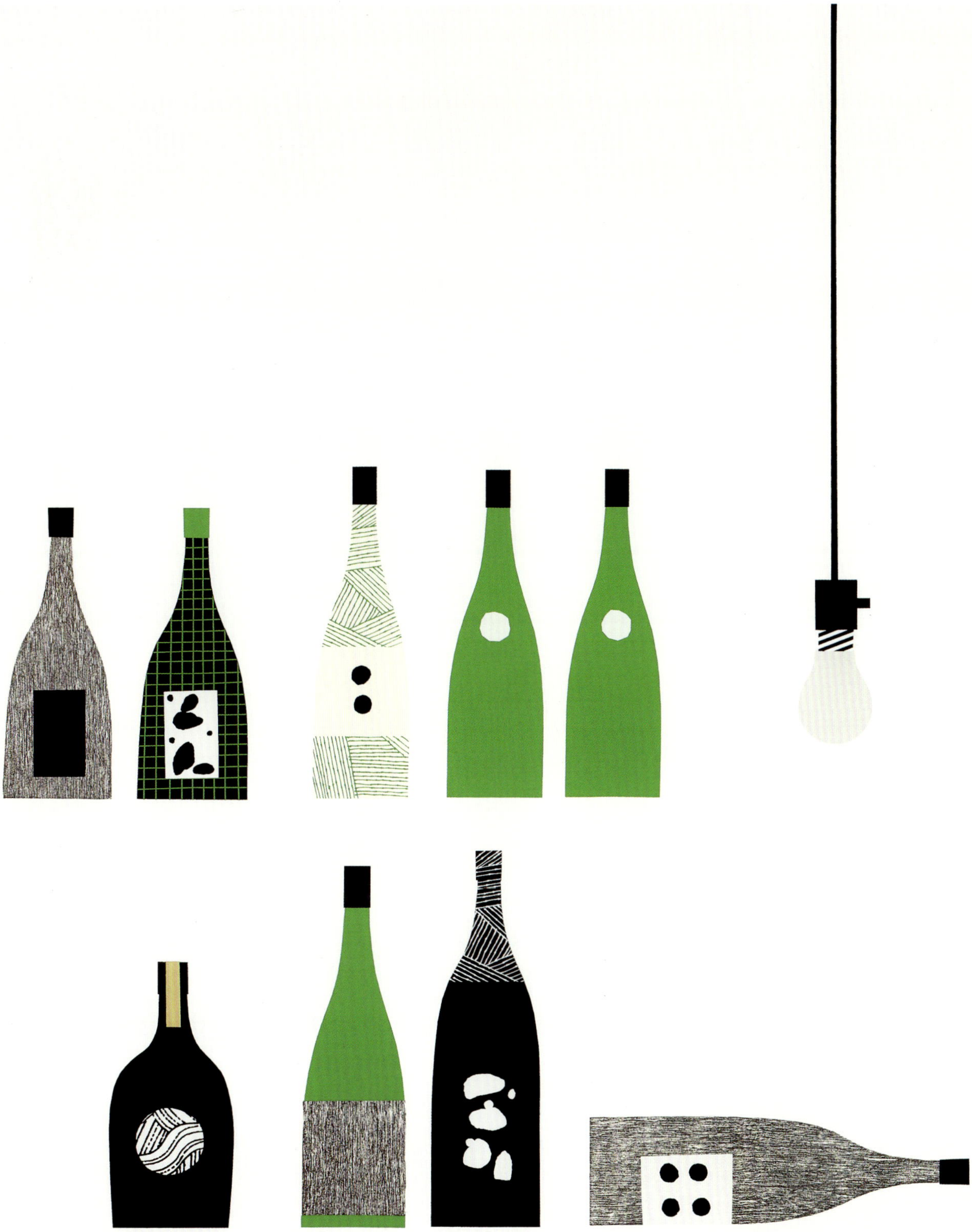

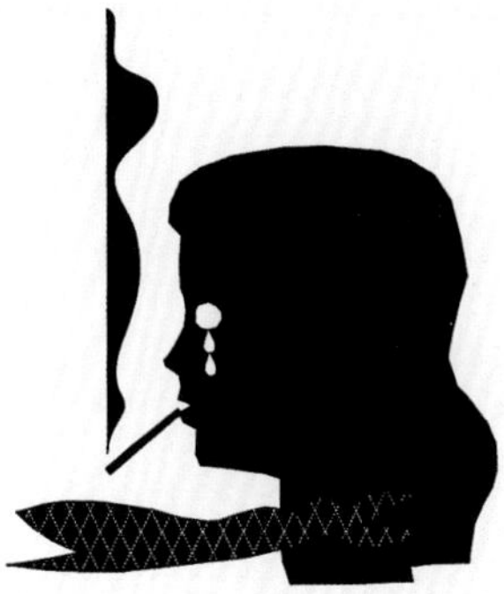

People leave therapy because they've hit an issue they're not able to deal with.
People leave therapy because they're unmotivated and not committed.
People leave therapy because they've finished.

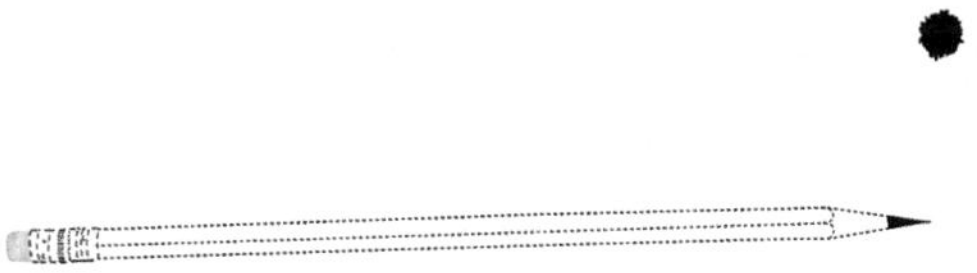

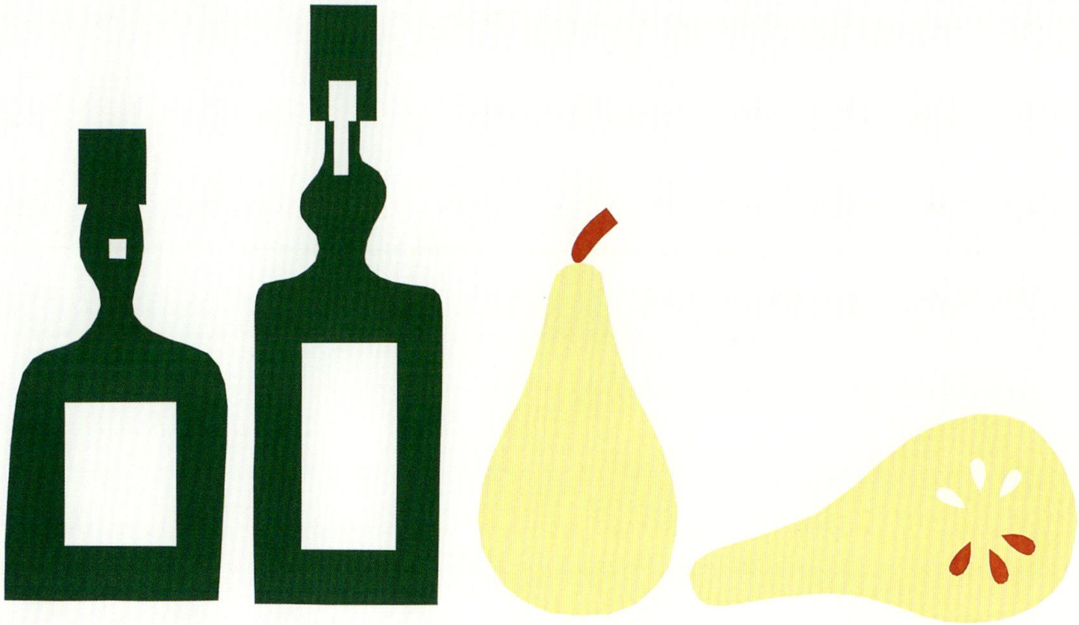

You catch yourself standing in the check-out line. Embarrassed for yourself. Our definition of art so progressive and yet. Here you are. Buying art supplies at the art supply store. In front of you the undergraduate with a shopping list. Behind you the retired hobbyist. Is this really any job for an adult? Can you really speak of what you do without cringing? A grown man talking about his feelings. When you're introduced to your friends' friends how can you begin to explain what you do?

The fruit goes from rock hard to rotten with no space in between. You hesitate to throw it out. Reminding yourself how much you paid for these exotic vegetables. A fridge full of disintegrating cheese. Of yogurt you consider eating well past its expiration date. A half empty vodka bottle in a narrow frosted cave of an icebox. A couple of frozen chickens you forgot to thaw.

Next to your bed a mountain of half read books. Ambitions abandoned. Introductions read twice. Dog-eared thoughts set aside. After a day spent putting out fires, how could you not drink. Not watch television.

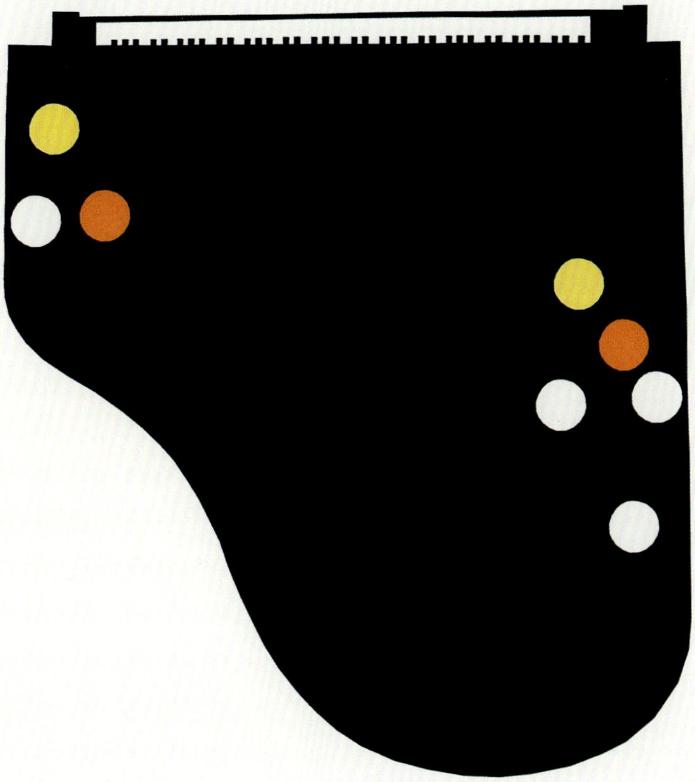

Guess. No guess again. Think back. No that's not even close. Remember when I told you I did something I shouldn't have done? In New York. That guy in the piano bar? Yeah. Well I did. I fucked him. And he's here tonight. And you were right. He *is* the author.

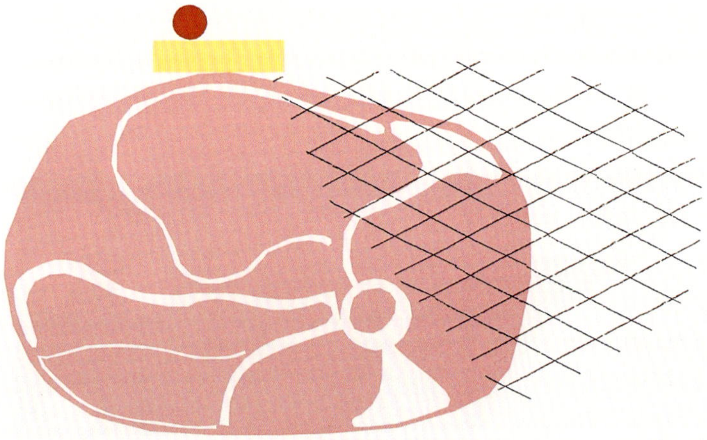

Halfway across the intersection you catch yourself mid-thought.
The unfinished plate. The second house. A too tight watch. A tap on the shoulder.
He wouldn't dare. He hasn't the nerve. This is my sand castle.

His plane lands around seven. When he arrives we've been waiting an hour or more. He's been drinking all day but he pretends it's his first. He tells us how he sat next to this very successful third-rate actor. About dinner the night before in Shanghai with a museum director and how they shared a similar anxiety concerning their future roles.

And now his hand indiscreetly touches yours. Reaching for more salt. Coughing when he asks if you like the wine. After dinner someone suggests charades. You decline and sit at the piano. Adjusting your incidental music to follow the game of frustrated mutes and spastic trivia. A cheap *Lolita*, a blunt *Razor's Edge*.

In bed at night we revisit the day's conversations. Waiting for the light. Hoping the morning isn't a myth.

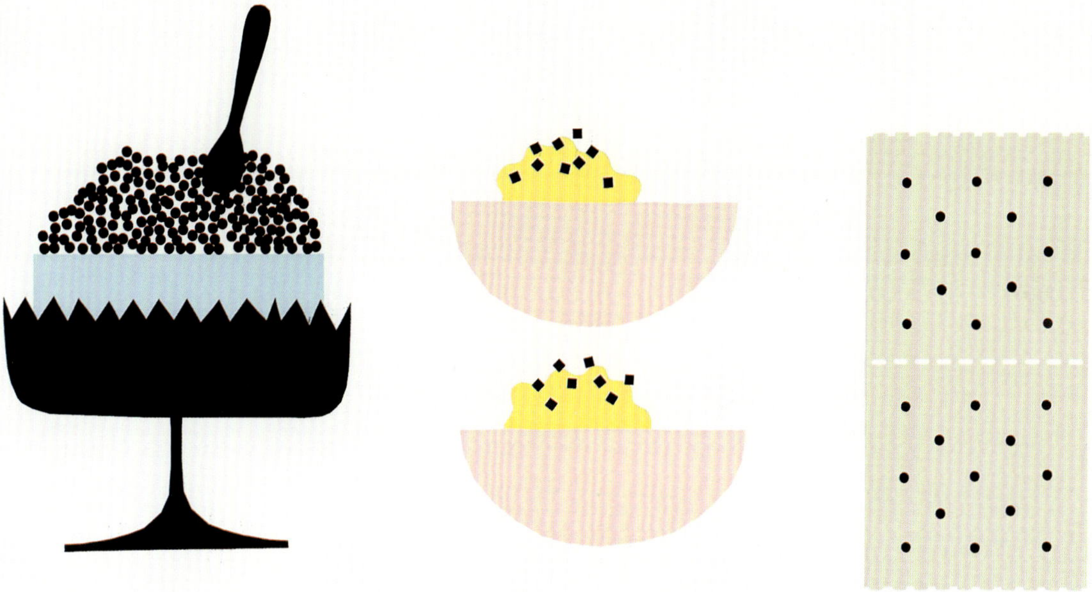

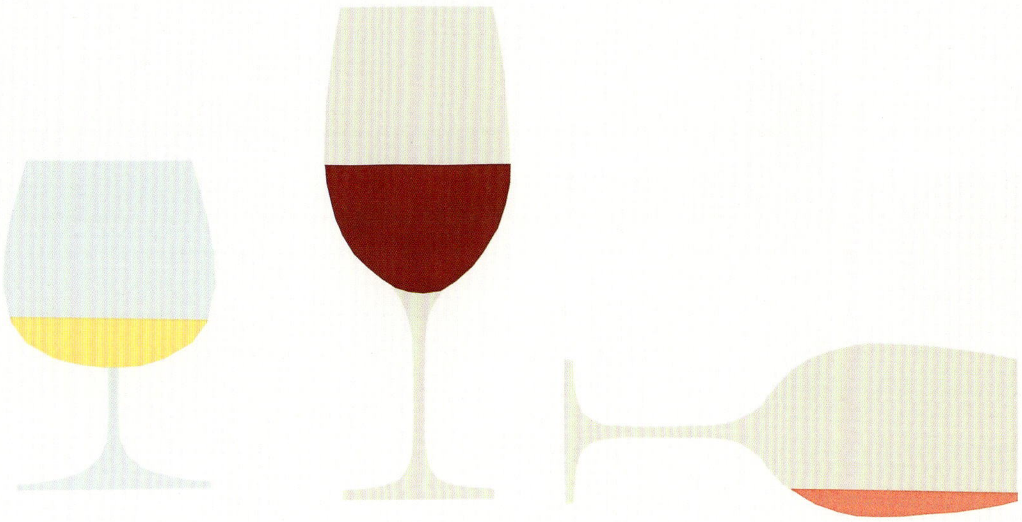

Before we begin. I'd like to thank everyone who made this evening possible. First there's ... whose countless hours and faith in this project... And ... who took the bullet when... And ... whose selflessness opened many doors once closed. And of course ... who knew what questions to ask and which to avoid, who provided the rent when there was none. And to the late ... you are in all our thoughts tonight.

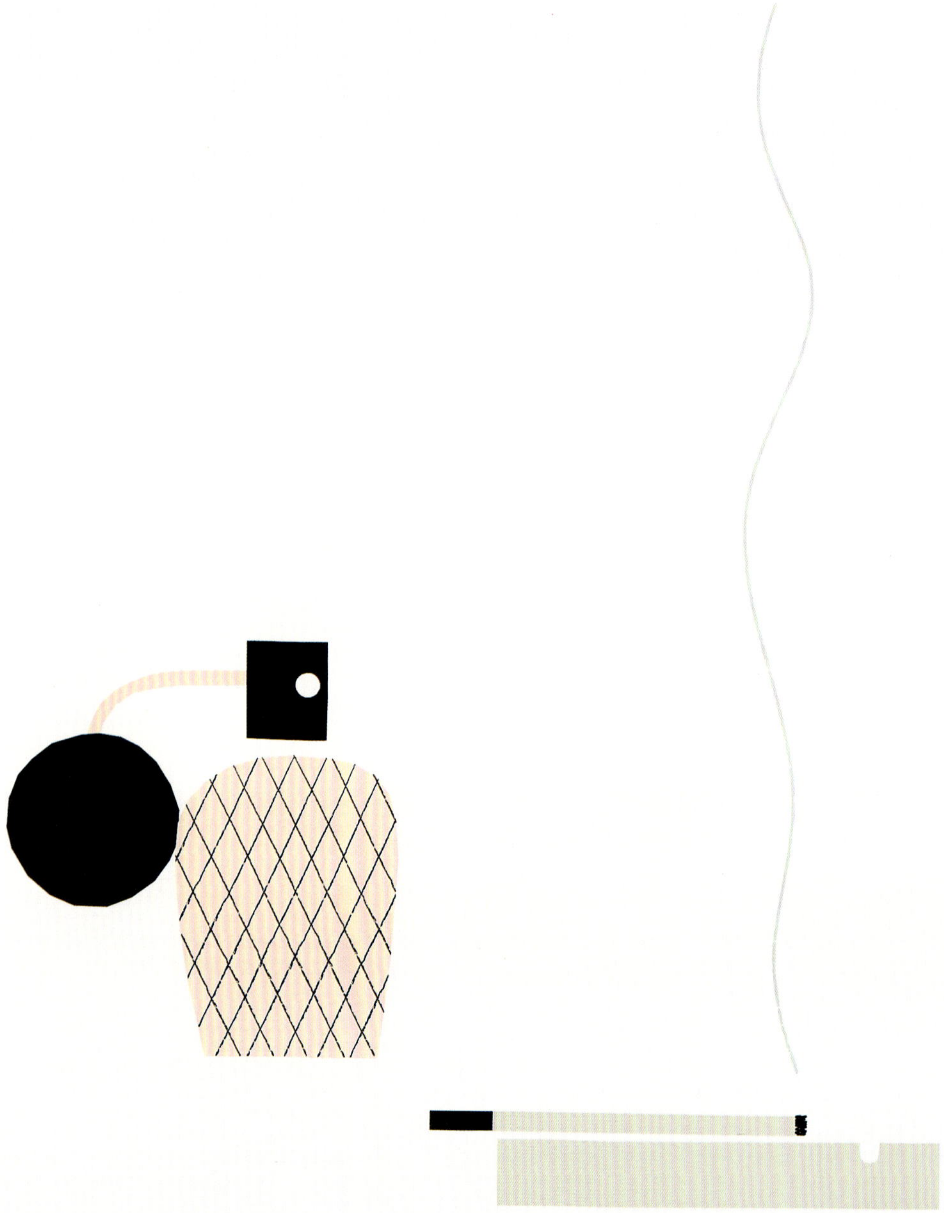

Finish your drink. We're leaving.

Being polite is key to living in a major metropolitan center. Whether it's consideration when hailing a cab, letting people exit before you enter, or not chewing gum in public. It's important. But you might also consider that wearing fur is offensive and obnoxious to most. Or that wearing an expensive suit but not shaving is patronizing. And never ever start a sentence with...

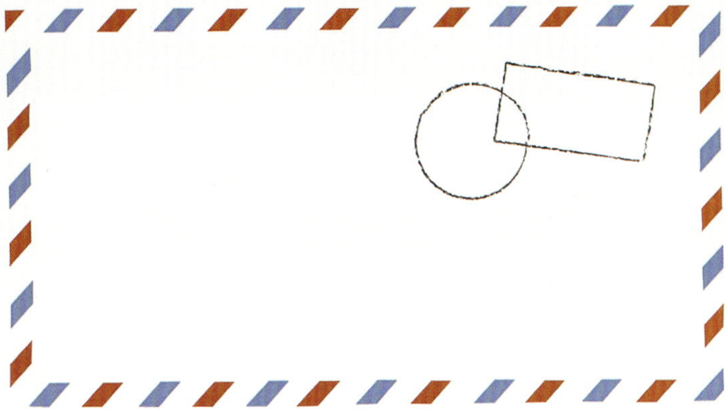

That's funny. I was sure I had locked the front door when we left.

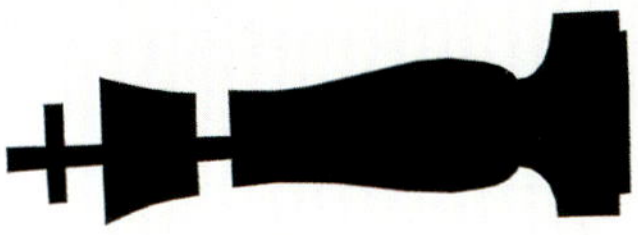

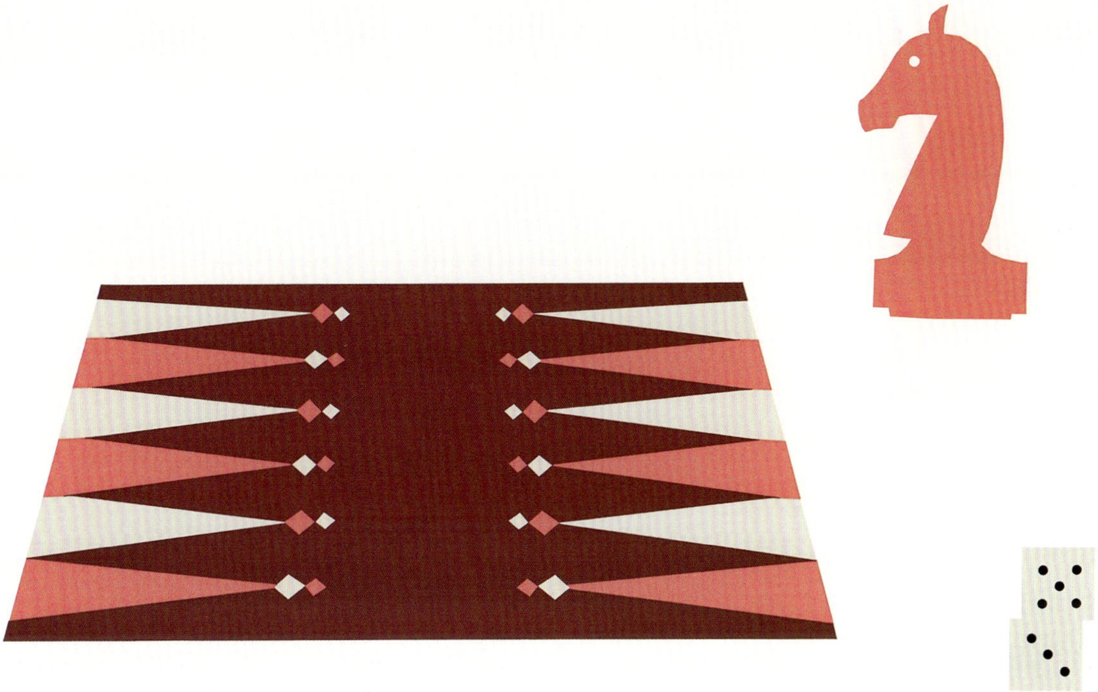

Kids don't give it away for free. Steer the boat away from the shore.
Everything you have counts. Everything they offer costs. Condoms are but ...
These nights, foggy notions. When they say it doesn't hurt - they lie.

More than you know.

To Say the Very Least

Matthew Brannon

To Say the Very Least

ART GALLERY OF YORK UNIVERSITY

A publication in conjunction with the exhibition:
Matthew Brannon: Try & Be Grateful
an AGYU Founders Presentation.
January 31 – April 1, 2007

agYU
Art Gallery of York University
4700 Keele St, Toronto ON M3J 1P3 Canada

The Art Gallery of York University is supported by York University, the Canada Council for the Arts, the Ontario Arts Council, and the City of Toronto through the Toronto Arts Council.

Original cover artwork by Matthew Brannon
Book design by Paul Wagner
This book is typeset in Stempel Garamond

Printed and bound in Canada by Transcontinental Litho-Acme

Available through
D.A.P./Distributed Art Publishers
155 Sixth Avenue, 2nd Floor
New York, NY 10013
TEL 212-627-1999 FAX 212-627-9484

Canada Council for the Arts Conseil des Arts du Canada

ONTARIO ARTS COUNCIL
CONSEIL DES ARTS DE L'ONTARIO

torontoartscouncil
An arm's length body of the City of Toronto

Library and Archives Canada Cataloguing in Publication
Matthew Brannon : to say the very least / introduction by Philip Monk.
Catalogue of an exhibition held at the Art Gallery of York University,
Toronto, Ont., Jan. 31–Apr. 1, 2007.
Includes index.
ISBN 978-0-921972-50-1
1. Brannon, Matthew, 1971- —Exhibitions. 1. York University (Toronto, Ont.).
Art Gallery II. Title: To say the very least.

N6537.B6826A4 2008 709.2
C2008-900983-5

Contents

More Than You Know

Philip Monk

Reader, if I told you, what would you make of the gift from artist to author of a copy of Sigmund Freud's *Civilization and Its Discontents*? Would it be admission of the artist's analytical sessions? A key to unlock the content of his pictures: a clue to both iconography and autobiography in his works? Or perhaps the answer to Brannon's question, "Why are people their own worst enemies?" If Freud answers this question, from this very book and others, Brannon does not transpose psychoanalysis's solutions to entitle his enterprise. His work still expresses a lack not a solution in its uncertain treading of the line between success and failure, concealment and exposure. Nevertheless, with Freud as a reference, we expect, at the least, that what underlies Brannon's prints is visible to see—and read—as symptoms on the surface of their artifact. For in the artifice of Brannon's prints, it is always a matter of seeing and reading, literally and in that order.

Although a slim mass-market paperback, this particular edition of Freud is singular. As part of Penguin Books *Great Ideas* series, it has been treated specially with an embossed cover on which the author's name and book title have been elegantly overprinted in black and red type. Brannon's gift thus hints at his own letterpress prints in an attempt perhaps not so much to explain his work but to egregiously assert its worth by mimetic rivalry. That is, if in the end he really felt himself worthy of such a comparison.

Passed from hand to hand like a cultural fetish, this book is token of a secret sharing invisible to scrutiny or sight. A gift, however, we have to admit, is no key. Receiving it, what would *I* have to admit here in order to write about Matthew Brannon? Or to be read? Would I have to confess, for instance, that I am writing this drunk?... deceptively?...*self*-deceptively?...or with malice? Whatever the case, I would not have the resources Brannon commands, which are given, in fact, in and by the very medium of his artwork: printmaking. What was receptive to touch in the private transmission between Matthew and me becomes the imprint of a very public presentation in the artist's work.

This is a story of mastery and failure, elegance and embarrassment. Up or down, in or out, no one comes out unscathed.

The Tractable Matthew Brannon

> Of course all life is a process of breaking down, but the blows that do the dramatic side of the work—the big sudden blows that come, or seem to come, from outside—the ones you remember and blame things on and, in moments of weakness, tell your friends about, don't show their effect all at once. There is another sort of blow that comes from within—that you don't feel until it's too late to do anything about it, until you realize with finality that in some regard you will never be as good a man again. The first sort of breakage seems to happen quick—the second kind happens almost without your knowing it but is realized suddenly indeed.
>
> —F. Scott Fitzgerald, *The Crack-Up*

Everything takes place on the surface, or just *under* it in Brannon's work, just as everything there is public or takes place *in* public. We shall try to find the relation between these two statements—and their two correlates—as together they define Brannon's work.

By public, first of all I mean not only that these prints are exposed in exhibition but also that they assume public forms. That is, they not only mimic genres but also are generic in their very use of word and image following the models of advertisements and posters, acquiring their easy elegance from the history of design. Take some of the earliest exemplars: *Sick Decisions* and *House of Rot* (both 2004). *Sick Decisions* and *House of Rot* reproduce movie posters of the 'B' or horror variety. Yet, Brannon's posters advertise only themselves or advertise only their titles, not any actual movie. Their referential function is short-circuited: there is no other product they send us to. Rather, they identify their own contents, which then must be interpreted according to their titles. Contents are given by a series of phrases that occupy the lower band of the print consistent with the placement of movie poster credits. Names of the production company, director, screenwriter, stars and co-stars, etc., have been oddly replaced by phrases such as, "A Frustrated Power Production—A Desperate Appeal Release—Sick Decisions—STARRING—Good Prison Visit—The Guilt Which Organizes Your Fear—Abuse of Education—Misplaced Trust—Not for Lack of Funds—", etc.

Are these collections of phrases symptomatic of "sick decisions" and "houses of rot" or are they merely the compilations of a smart-ass wordsmith who is keen "to brand or market phrases"? Who yet can say? In a 2006 interview, Brannon said, "I seek a play with words that is both specific in meaning and conversely teetering with inappropriate reception. But most often the poetry takes the form of a list, a roll call, or credit to one's delusional life."[1] Disregarding Brannon's "but," we might wonder whether, teetering, inappropriate reception is not only intimately linked to specific meaning but to the language dynamics of delusion, as well.

At any rate, these prints gather together images, titles, and phrases that play within ready-made genres—the horror picture in particular rather than the movie poster per se—which unite the individual (that is, sick decisions) to what Freud calls the "family romance" (that is, house of rot). (This gothic character is further exaggerated in the similarly structured works mimicking movie posters, *Premature Ejaculation* and *Grotesque Desperate* from 2005.) Not the typical haunted house, but, as we expect, the family home is not far behind—literally. It is obscured by the overlay of decorative motifs: circles of scrollwork as if details of an ornate ironwork gate through which the screened-back images of suburban homes can be glimpsed. Language, too, acts equally to obscure the background image but not through any imprecision of meaning or reference: both decoration and titles alike draw the eye to the surface. It is a case, as Derrida says, of the text "not there to say the saying inasmuch as it withholds from seeing."[2]

Seeing and reading are implicated in one another, but not in any immediately legible way. Other than the interjected titles, illustrations command attention. In the hierarchy of presentation, other text is secondary and usually appears below. Because of the texts' placement and point size, we have to bend over in front of a print to read them. Yet, writing here, I take the easy path or the unconscious route of treating Brannon's texts as the content of his work. Here is the first contradiction of my text. Then again, how does one write about illustration or decoration, which are usually secondary to any presentation? These elements, traditionally *parerga*, which include the works' titles, infiltrate centre stage. Here we have the second and third contradictions, but now of the work. However, we will never be sure where centre stage is in these works, indeed, what is central and what is peripheral, what is on view and what puts to view. (To remind ourselves of the "insistent atopics of the *parergon*: neither work [*ergon*] nor outside the work {*hors d'oeuvres*}, neither inside nor outside, neither above nor below, it disconcerts any opposition but does not remain indeterminate and it *gives rise* to the work. It is no longer merely around the work. That which it puts in place—the instances of the frame, the title, the signature, the legend, etc.—does not stop disturbing the *internal* order of discourse on painting, its works, its commerce, its evaluations, its surplus-values, its speculation, its law, and its hierarchies."[3])

The series *Loss of Words*, *Distraction Becomes You*, *Submission*, and *Drunk Baptism* (all 2004) exploit a less obvious form of signage, namely wine bottle labels (which themselves have their own history of typographic discernment). The embossed labels are only part of an overall illustrational schema, along with other accoutrements that drinking signifies (and effects consumption supposedly originate): boa feathers, champagne flutes, overturned wine bottles, broken glasses, and evanescent bubbles that prick the paper support. The language of the titles, for instance, "distraction becomes you" and "submission," might be seductions and slogans for perfume advertising campaigns more than for liquor consumption, but they are turned, in the contrary logic of the *pharmakon*, towards ill consequences and unpardonable acts. For instance, in *Submission*, "9 glasses later, everything you say will come back to hurt you." We might think that this language is turned around and against the apparatus of its appearance, that it counters advertising as a critique. But it is just as imagined or imaginary as advertising, and more self-delusional perhaps than corporate sell. Each print houses a little scenario, or back-story, easily overlooked as they are disguised typographically as faux wine labels and then, moreover, reversed in part. The label for *Distraction Becomes You* reads as if an obligatory government warning, "champagne headache/web-like distrust," and then in reverse type, "unable to feel or care or make decisions." Similarly, *Drunk Baptism* reads, "vin fin de table de God/the fear which organizes your guilt," followed in reverse type by "everything I want, you have." In the ambiguity of address here, we have to yet wonder who so authoritatively is speaking and to whom?

The deviation of the text is not disingenuous. Reversal obscures only what is in plain sight. It admits what is difficult to say personally or publicly. This device is a guarded moment of truth telling. Irony serves the same veiled purpose. So does the decorum of decoration. Adolph Loos said ornament is a crime, but the perfect crime would be décor. Purloined letters would be invisible there. What could an acute observer of society hide within the invisible visibility of decoration that would reflect a culture unaware back to itself?

In the last few years there has been a widespread return in print advertising from photography to illustration, which has particularly played on the retro styles and fashions of the 1950s. Brannon's prints evoke illustrative styles of the past as if they were, for instance, decorations to cookbooks or cocktail manuals but now enlarged and having inverted their secondary relationship to the main text. This domestic turn and suburban return has an uncomfortable edge in Brannon's hands: kitchen knives, severed goosenecks and cocks' heads, interspersed with scatterings of pinecones and needles in themselves are innocent enough without need to refer to a possible castration complex. (Freud, of course, was popularized in America in the 1950s.) But as in Douglas Sirk's 1950s Hollywood melodramas, domestic artifacts and décor are symbols of societal constraints and vain achievements (such as his famous framed mirrors and trophies). Another of Brannon's print series from 2004, thus, says it all in one of its title: *Country Club Upset*. Indeed, the reverse text in these prints précis mini-melodramas of derailed individuals as if *TV Guide* entries: *Disappointed Critic*: "diet pill paranoia & plastic trophies"; *End of the Family Line*: "delusional self-importance builds"; *Limp Consideration*: "career train wreck alcoholic workaholic seeks same."

"The million-dollar question I appreciate," Brannon has said, is "Why are people their own worst enemies?" Then as if offering a compendium of the content of his work, he goes on to list "topics which satellite around this question involve careerism, sexual misadventure, substance abuse, alcoholism, poor finances, poor parenting."[4] His images, though, betray none of these issues. How could a design of coral and tropical fish illustrate career failure or personal pathologies as suggested by the titles *Fatal Career Misstep* or *Belligerent Euphoria* (2005)? Their respective texts explain nothing of the conditions or consequences, nor do their lists of phrases themselves resolve into any coherent narrative any more than Brannon's compendium quoted at the start of this paragraph. At a stretch, they might indicate a cluster of symptoms, but usually the lists collect different orders or registers of language use.

While we might see Brannon as a successor to earlier work on the social constructs of masculinity (Richard Prince) or the confusion of corporate and sociopathic behaviour in American culture (Cady Noland), he belongs to a longer line from which his work receives its drunk baptism. At least, the work, not the artist's life, takes its themes from this tradition, which stems from the "literary drunkenness" of Edgar Allan Poe, to use Baudelaire's phrase about this unhappy, failed American artist. Poe's career is emblematic of the constraints of a commercial culture on its arts and the compromises artists need make, extending even to genres they work in—or invent. On the East Coast, the relationships of writers and artists to Madison Avenue and on the West Coast to Hollywood, especially since the 1950s, have spawned their own genre in books and movies. (A subcategory includes the relation of artists to the domestic in the melodramas of suburban commuter culture.)

We could very crudely characterize these relationships for artists by the following diagram:

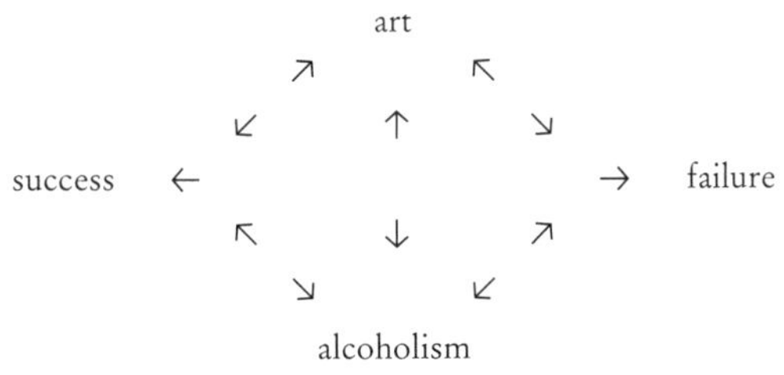

In this schema, the extremes of success and failure and those of art and alcoholism are not necessarily correlated (art and success or alcoholism and failure). In fact, we are not charting structural oppositions or terminal positions but a perceptual process that is not necessary overtly visible. This process is not apparent in the image but occurs in a narrative or happens during a monologue a character tells him- or herself in an excoriating moment of self-realization and confession. Thus, the two prints both titled *The last thing you remember was staring at the little white tiles* (2006), with their respective his and hers matched set of trophies (or are they king or queen chess-pieces?), now read differently as scenarios rather than just lists of phrases. Something similarly happens in both cases to reveal the individuals to themselves and to us. Here is the "his" version:

> —WALL TO WALL MIRRORS IN A PRIVATE BATHROOM AT A PARTY YOU NEED TO LEAVE—PALM TREES BRUSH THE WINDOWS—OUTSIDE THE SOUND OF INSECTS—THE CREDIT CARD DOESN'T HAVE YOUR NAME ON IT—SLIDE THE MIRROR RIGHT—SCAN THE PRESCRIPTIONS—SLIDE THE MIRROR LEFT—NOTE THE MOUTHWASH AND BAND AIDS—AN ASHED CIGARETTE INSIDE A FORTY FIVE DOLLAR SCENTED CANDLE—BLACK SOAP IN THE SHAPE OF A DOG—PERFUME & POWDER BOTTLES—LOOK AT YOUR GRAY FACE—RUN YOUR HANDS UNDER COLD WATER—RUN YOUR TONGUE OVER YOUR TEETH—TASTE BLOOD—BREATH IN AND FLINCH—YOUR COCK NOW HALF ITS SIZE—SWALLOW BITTER PHLEGM—FIGHT THE PANIC—FIGHT THE NAUSEA—THIS ISN'T PART OF YOUR JOB DESCRIPTION—THIS ISN'T THE WAY IT ENDS—THIS IS THE AWFUL LAST OF IT—HOLD THE SINK ON THE WAY TO THE FLOOR—LAY YOUR HEAD IN THE PISS SOAKED RUG—TRY TO FOCUS—WAVES OF HEAT & PRESSURE—SOMEONE IS KNOCKING—EVERYONE IS LAUGHING—WISH THAT CANDLE WAS OUT—

"*Whatever could have happened for things to have come to this?*" Gilles Deleuze and Félix Guattari ask in relation to F. Scott Fitzgerald's essay *The Crack-Up*. They continue, "It is better to think of it as an affair of perception: you enter a room and perceive something as already there, as just having happened, even though it has not yet been done. Or you know that what is in the process of happening is happening for the last time, it's already over with. You hear an 'I love you' you know is the last one. Perceptual semiotics. God, whatever could have happened, even though everything is and remains imperceptible, and in order for everything to be and remain imperceptible forever?"[5]

Something has happened, but this "something happened," for us, is inflected by the telling. Phrases accumulate as if they are edits of film shots not just the consciousness of the character. Descriptions become imperatives of seeing: "slide the mirror right—scan the prescriptions—note the mouthwash and band aids." In this crossover of film and writing, writing shades the situation with a tinge of noir. The genre precipitates the "action" or the fall, which is the imperceptible change. On the model of film noir, we could call Brannon's works décor noir—perceptual semiotics obscured by decorative motifs.

Given this stylization of the text by genre, we realize that we are not dealing with individuals but character types. These types are defined by genre. No individual is confessing here—certainly not the artist/author, even if we are tempted to attribute "wanted to talk about abusive lifestyles—wanted to address how it all goes wrong" from *Raw Bar* to him. The expressions are already cultural and commonplace. (Even though Brannon invents them, they have the ring of the ready-made with their immediately recognizable connotations.)

Noir heroes are already on a downward slide, even before a precipitous new turn of events. Often living on the borderline between inside and outside society and operating, like artists, between the high life and riff raff, they are well poised to observe the corruptions and illusions of society, once they have seen past their own lack of innocence. The noir crisis of consciousness, sometimes precipitated by a temporal disjunction (waking up beside a dead man not knowing how you got there), is the closest we have in our culture to the past function of the *memento mori*. In the past, these paintings, which allegorized death and sin in luxurious images such as table settings of overflowing flowers, fruit, fish, and fowl or simple juxtapositions of a skull and candle, reminded us of our mortality: remember you will die. With their ordinary domestic images disguising some other content, Brannon's prints address our guilty consciousness or guilty identifications through a subtext that is only revealed secondarily and as a crisis to the self. Thus, *Slut Best Friend* with its shrimp cocktail, *More Autopsy Than Diagnosis* with its lobster and tableware, and *Don't Call, Don't Even Write* with its side table décor of lamp, horse figurine, and clump of coral (all 2006). Thus, the turn within the text in *Slut Best Friend* from "—go to restaurants few can afford—collect art—breed miniature dogs—buy clothes few could wear—attempt hardcore—" to "—beg for another chance —once exotic now tedious—always the alcoholic—even in sobriety—even on days off—especially tonight—"; or, the turn within consciousness of *Bad Manners* (2008): "Halfway across the intersection you catch yourself mid-thought. The unfinished plate. The second house. A too tight watch. A tap on the shoulder. He wouldn't dare. He hasn't the nerve. This is my sand castle."

In such genre paintings, we do not look into their images as if through a window but see ourselves reflected back in the objects they depict. They are otherwise known as *vanitas* or vanity paintings and find their model, of course, in mirrors. It's not surprising then to see Brannon's prints reproducing this relationship as if our image is only temporarily absent in the open door of a vanity cabinet, the contents of toiletries and pills exposed: as in *Pulling Out*, the appropriately titled *Not So Young*, or *The Men in Your Life* with its skeletal hand menacing its toilette scene (all 2007).

Through this unavoidable daily image practice, a society binds an individual to it not so much only by its products as through its significations. Advertising takes up this *vanitas* mirror model, reflecting our desires back to us—and not without necessarily suppressing the guilt factor. Indeed, advertising often plays up excess without guilt, or excess beyond guilt. (See *Steak Dinner*, 2007: "—This year tell her you love her all over again—with a grab bag of diamonds—with mouthfuls of caviar—with your rent in clothes—a credit card of hotel rooms—stockings—champagne—plane tickets—and a soft slap on her bare ass—") Don't expect Brannon to perform a salutary critique countering advertising through its own language. Advertising supplies the language model for all occasions. *Pigs, Like Us* repeats the formula of *Steak Dinner*: "—they had to pump her stomach—amazing what they found—among the arugula, watercress, blue-fin tuna, age-dried steak—there it is—your heart—and look ... a bunch of razor blades—little light bulbs—cocaine—little travel bottles—anti-depressants—your old untouched job application—"

Language holds this list together containing this odd assortment in some sort of equivalency of ingestion. It's an equivalency commodities otherwise share, that is, when they are displayed in shop windows. These prints not only mirror mirrors but their equivalent: shop windows. And in mirroring shop windows, they mirror our culture. Here we find all we desire and more... more than you know—even humiliation and abjection. Culture holds all these together, civilization and its discontents, not as an accumulation only of products but of symptoms, as well. A recent print depicts a hanging shark, its exposed stomach a collection of bottles, bones, and skeletal hands. Would it surprise you to know that it's title is *The Profits and Losses of Biting the Hand that Feeds* and that it premiered at a prestigious art fair?

The Intractable Matthew Brannon

> The inward directed craving for destruction mostly eludes our perception, of course, unless it is tinged with eroticism.
>
> —Sigmund Freud, *Civilization and Its Discontents*

Calculating the profits and losses of biting the hand that feeds you is risky business. It can end in success or failure. At the same time, it makes a game of success and failure. You can't see this tightrope Brannon walks because of how *you* participate in the game. The way you participate is how you automatically attribute success or failure or have it attributed to you. Walking the tightrope, Brannon teeters now inside, now outside the system, anticipating the risks of biting the hand that feeds him.[6] We are mistaken to think that, at any time, he stands altogether *outside* the system making a critique of it: he is a *full* participant. So much there depends on chance. He's calculated the odds in how things stand right now. You can't offend collectors with work today. They'll clamour and compete for it even if it insults them to their face. Brannon has staked his success on this. Can you trust the man? Or what he says? At the least, you would have to interpret everything he says as if he was a patient on a psychoanalyst's couch and then qualify his aggression.

Yet, Brannon only reveals the system by exposing himself. He masters the system to do so. This is the reason for the panoplied effects of his work: the care—or control—he asserts in framing devices from invitations and posters to hanging systems and exhibition design. I've implied that parergonal effects also enter *into* the works themselves but now to other effect than mastery. Everyone knows that printmaking is a debased medium in the hierarchy of art making. Brannon makes it otherwise so elegant. For such mastery in a debased medium, he would have to unmaster and debase himself. At least, it appears that the work's process is (a) debasing.

Over the couch or on it, Brannon would have it both ways. That is, he would always only repeat what was already in his own work. Above and below. Over and under the surface. In "public" and in "private." And between the two.

Symptoms are telling, that is, if we can separate public and private and not see what is advertised in public (not just as advertising but *as* public, the *res publica*) as symptoms that otherwise condemn the individual. Symptoms are secreted in the individual. Nevertheless, this is a public affair. Matthew Brannon makes it so. He only repeats in public what is already given there.

Over the couch, obviously, as decoration, and *on* it in analysis. The print splits itself in two. It is subject to this system of division and, in necessarily splitting itself, it casts part of itself below. In so doing, however, it also represses this division.

On the one hand, with the decorative print over the couch, Brannon takes advantage of the situation by using décor to expose the system, but only formally, that is to say, by the work's elegant mask. The artwork expands out to the system's support: from the frame, to the context, to the institution, to the market. Yet only by exposing himself *below* do these parergonal effects return *in* the work to characterize the system as a whole.[7]

But on the other hand, in the ways of the couch—that is, on it, so to speak, as the subject in analysis—this exposure is guarded and devious, although it (he) tells its (his) truth through some deviancy. Deviancy merely means displacement, not deception, perhaps only a displacement of where to look or expect to look. The image, as always, is both central and distracting. But lower down, secondarily and in its secondary place, text debases itself, meanwhile debasing the individual. Whatever is said there, however low, would still be in your face.

A print is pliable; it takes an impression. Paper is tractable to an impression offering just so much resistance in its reception of an imprint. Not just receptive, printmaking is an articulated medium. Articulation disappears in the process, though, in the mirror of a print's making—from a plate, platen, or stone—leaving only an image. Although at first, in Brannon's case, only an imprint takes. At first take. Then the singular impression is repeated in colour to reveal the image. The impression does not disappear altogether from sight as if repressed from consciousness, as in the mystic writing-pad. The effects of the operation slide under *and* down, as if there were two subjectiles of one work supporting and relating image and text.[8] What falls beneath or what is only thrown down below or beneath would rise in the work capturing our attention like a slap on the face—or worse.

I can't help but think of another very different artist who said shit to the world, Antonin Artaud who wrote: "*you will realize/from my maladroit drawings/but so crafty,/and so adroit,/that say SHIT to this world.*" Derrida glosses this statement with a discussion of Artaud's drawings thus:

> To *throw* something right in someone's face, like an insult frank and straight and direct, addressed to this world with no detour, to spit at that face the figure of *excrement*, in a word, shit, that sums it all up: gestures, grammar, arithmetic, and the Kabbala that shits *at* the other and *on* the other. The crafty person, who comes to correct some wrong, is a sort of copula between the right of the *adroit* and the right of the awkward. The drawings are awkward because they are crafty, skillful, sly, adroit, indirect stratagems for plaguing this world with its norms and values, its expectations, its Art, its police, its psychiatry: in a word, its *rights*. Artaud is speaking to these sick rights to force them to say shit and saying it to those rights. *To* these rights, and *at* them, casting out the very word like excrement as well as excrement as a word. There would be a lot to say about the notions of address and law and rights, precisely, and the directions of the *throw* or the spurt [*le jet*], of the rejection [*le rejet*], the dejection, and the excrement. You can cast or spurt in all directions, whether with a projectile weapon or to send some gift, even some help. But sometimes it's enough to say "cast" or "throw" [*jeter*] in order to suggest the connotation of the cast or thrown away [*le déchet*] as it is rejected or abandoned. Usually, I throw on the floor anything that seems to me without value, or shoddy. But excrement, a perfectly shaped model of what is thus rejected downward, can also be of value as a weapon or as a present. And it can be thrown *upon* as well as *at*. At the other or upon the other. What receives excrement like that, for example right in the face [*la figure*] of its name, could be the surface of an underlying body, a subjectile in general,

> but we should also note that the subjectile was constituted in this world and in the traditional history of its Art as an excrement itself: what doesn't belong to the body of the *work* is found beneath it, an epigraph, a matter exterior and parergonal sometimes dropped.[9]

"Adroit" and "maladroit" are only other signifiers for terms by which we have considered Brannon's works. The truth Brannon tells of America would not be Artaud's in France, but the two artists resort to similar means with different vehemence to let their work have its effect.

The tractable Matthew Brannon would be the man of mastery, yet conforming to the system with all the signs merely of rebellion. He would offer what was for sale. The intractable Matthew Brannon would be otherwise. Maybe a bit too familiar to us. Where would we draw the intractable division between mastery and conformity, between, as *A Lot like Trash* has it, "a conservative version of radical—a radical version of conservative"? Where would *you* like it, reader: Right in the face?

NOTES

1. Rosa Vanina Pavone, "Innocent Accidental Unintentional Indulgent. Never. An Interview with Matthew Brannon," *Uovo* (April 2006), 150.

2. Jacques Derrida, *Given Time: 1. Counterfeit Money*, trans. Peggy Kamuf (Chicago and London: The University of Chicago Press, 1992), 121.

3. Jacques Derrida, "Passe-Partout," *The Truth in Painting*, trans. Geoff Bennington and Ian McLeod (Chicago and London: The University of Chicago Press, 1987), 9.

4. Pavone, 152.

5. Gilles Deleuze and Félix Guattari, *A Thousand Plateaus: Capitalism & Schizophrenia,* trans. Brian Massumi (Minneapolis: University of Minnesota Press, 1987), 194.

6. "Brannon straddles the same line between grandeur and misery, and does so just as knowingly—interested as he is in restaging those social intricacies composing the 'court' of our contemporary art world. The thirty-four-year-old artist's recent exhibition at the David Kordansky Gallery in Los Angeles opened with *Health Insurance*, 2005, a framed real-estate advertisement from the '70s featuring a melancholic 'swinger' leaning against the mantle inside his well-appointed digs, obligatory martini in hand. THE GOOD LIFE, reads the text: SUCCESS IN HIS OAKHURST TERRACE PENTHOUSE...AN INVESTMENT IN BEAUTY AND SECURITY.... This sinister appropriation, with ad lingo intact, would seem to swerve Richard Prince's paradigmatic late-'70s images of living rooms and men in suits into an even more blatant critique of the corporate fetish, one that finally is stripped of its flimsy allegorical armature when it is disclosed that Oakhurst Terrace is rumored to belong to one of Kordansky's most important collectors. With the incredible cost of the properties noted at the bottom of the image, the promise of both 'beauty and security' only corroborates the crasser aspects of the current speculative market on younger artists. Brannon's cynical take on the state of today's art world is underlined by his decision to cap the image with a headstone. If there's a joke here, it's on every one of us, artist included." Jan Tumlir, "Openings: Jan Tumlir on Matthew Brannon," *Artforum* (February 2006), 196.

7. "What constitutes them as *parerga* is not simply their exteriority as a surplus, it is the internal structural link which rivets them to the lack in the interior of the *ergon*. And this lack would be constitutive of the very unity of the *ergon*. Without this lack, the *ergon* would have no need of a *parergon*." Derrida, "Parergon," *The Truth in Painting*, 59–60.

8. "Following the injunction, we will no longer be able to separate the drawing from the writing: the writing in it and writing outside of it, apparently dealing with it.... We would like to *take account*, in sum, of two works and two subjectiles, two papers, one coming after the other and dealing with it, the one *on* which there would be held a discourse *about* the other, a 'commentary' dealing with the other. But this is not to be. The texts are different but inseparable, neither of the two is subjected or subordinated to the other, as its second. There are two subjectiles for one work, and in truth, two unique examples of the same event, absolutely different but indissociable. Is this even possible? But if it were not impossible, what would be the interest?" Jacques Derrida, "To Unsense the Subjectile," *The Secret Art of Antonin Artaud*, trans. Mary Ann Caws (Cambridge, Mass. And London, England: The MIT Press, 1998), 124.

9. Derrida, "To Unsense the Subjectile," 117–18.

Index

PAGE 3
More Autopsy Than Diagnosis, 2006
letterpress on paper
24 × 18 in. (61 × 45.7 cm)
edition of 1
COMPETITIVENESS REVEALS AN INSECURE CORE ONLY SATIATED BY OTHERS' PRAISE · LEFT WITH AN UNCEASING PRESSURE · THE HEAVILY GUARDED PECKING ORDER NEVER ALLOWS REST · THE TIGHTROPE WALK OF CONFIDENCE · A FEW VISUAL GIMMICKS MASK CONSERVATIVE, ILL THOUGHT OUT, DESPERATE PLEAS FOR ATTENTION

PAGE 5
My Mistake, 2008
letterpress on paper
22 × 16 in. (55.9 × 40.6 cm)
edition of 1
All we are and what we're not.

PAGE 7
Don't Call, Don't Even Write, 2006
letterpress on paper
38 × 29 in. (96.5 × 73.7 cm)
edition of 1
IT'S HARD TO SAY · I'M ASSUMING THE ANSWER WAS NO · DIDN'T SAY A WORD · THREW THAT RING IN THE TRASH · THE FRIENDS LEFT BEHIND · THE CHEAP SUBSTITUTES FOR TALENT · THE LATE NIGHTS & MISSED MEETINGS · THE COFFEE IN YOUR LAP · HOW IT SHOULD HAVE BEEN · HOW IT WAS · I DIDN'T WANT TO BE THE ONE TO TELL YOU

PAGE 9
Grey Poupon, 2008
letterpress on paper
22 × 16 in. (55.9 × 40.6 cm)
edition of 1
Just one more minute. I've already called the ambulance. You're going to make it. I know you are. And all those things I said, well I never meant them. You weren't the last person on my mind. And when I said … I was lying.

We study the wall label. Forming an image of the artist from a last name, birthplace & date of birth. From a title and a list of materials. He's younger than I thought. He's a she. She's actually from Europe. It's more than cardboard. It took him three years to make this. It's owned by what's his name.

PAGE 12–13
Try & Be Grateful, 2007
(installation view)
Art Gallery of York University

PAGE 15
Sick Decisions, 2004
silkscreen on paper
40 × 26 in. (101.2 × 66 cm)
edition of 10
FRUSTRATED POWER PRODUCTION · A DESPERATE APPEAL RELEASE · SICK DECISIONS · STARRING GOOD PRISON VISIT · THE GUILT WIHICH ORGANIZES YOUR FEAR · ABUSE OF EDUCATION · MISPLACED TRUST · NOT FOR LACK OF FUNDS · CO-STARRING · 25 YEARS OF VALUE, VIRTUE, & LEADERSHIP · THOSE WHO ENJOY CORRECTING OTHERS · VIDEOS ON VALIUM · POOR ATTEMPT AT THANK YOU · PAST YOUR BEST · GREAT TITLES FOR BAD BOOKS · PITIFUL PORTION · A NAME YOU REGRET · MUSIC BY VICTIM DANSE & TURN PALE · SCREENPLAY BY 101 UNANSWERED PHONE CALLS · ORIGINAL STORY BY BRET EASTON ELLIS'S HEAD ON A PLATE · PRODUCED BY LAST ATTEMPT AT LOVE & SOFT TEETH · DIRECTED BY EXHAUSTED BLOOD & IMITATION SALT

PAGE 17
House of Rot, 2004
silkscreen on paper
40 × 26 in. (101.2 × 66 cm)
edition of 10
A FRUSTRATED POWER PRODUCTION · A DECADENT MEDICATION RELEASE · HOUSE OF ROT · STARRING · UNCHECKED CONFIDENCE · ASSPLAY · 7 YEARS IN ONE NIGHT · PARLOR OF REGRET · DIVORCE MAGAZINE · CO-STARRING · EFFORT JUDGEMENT · REVEALING COMMENT · COMPLAIN TO UNDERSTAND · LAYERS UPON LAYERS OF FAT · WASTED CONTACT & EXPENSIVE ADVICE · DEFINED BY WHAT YOU HATE · PSYCHOTROPIC GIFT · BELLIGERENT EUPHORIA · KNEE- JERK NEGATIVITY · MUSIC BY CARPETED QUOTE WITH PERVERSE AMBITION · SCREENPLAY BY DIET COKE & VODKA · ORIGINAL STORY BY BLACK AM. EX. · PRODUCED BY NIGHT SWEATS & SLUG BAIT · DIRECTED BY LOVE UNDER WILL UNDER STRESS

PAGE 18
Premature Ejaculation, 2005
silkscreen on paper
30 × 22 in. (76.2 × 55.9 cm)
edition of 5
TORN APART PICTURES PRESENTS · A NEVER THAT LASTS FOREVER RELEASE · A HOLLOW NEST FILM · PREMATURE EJACULATION · STARRING · THE DISAPPOINTMENTS OF KENNETH ANGER · THE SMELL OF DEATH · GREY WOLVES SIPPING CHIANTI · THE GRUESOME GUESTS · A SADISTIC DJ · CO-STARRING · BRUISED ARMS AND WET CIGARETTES · PARTY WITH YOUR PUBERTY · BROKEN GATES · PASS OUT WALLET DUMP · WET STEAMING PANT MEAT · PRODUCED BY · FANS OF FAKES AND FANS OF FILTH · CREDIBILITY GAINS - CONFIDENCE LOST · SWOLLEN ACTOR · ORIGINAL MUSIC BY · SEMEN OF SEVEN SICK SERVANTS · WRITTEN BY · RECREATIONAL DRUG ABUSE · BASED ON THE NOVEL · TROPICAL ITCH ICE PICK · DIRECTED BY· SINK FULL OF BLOOD

PAGE 19
Grotesque Desperate, 2005
silkscreen on paper
30 × 22 in. (76.2 × 55.9 cm)
edition of 5
AN INABILITY TO MAKE DECISIONS PRESENTS · AN ATROCIOUS IRRITANT PRODUCTION OF · GROTESQUE DESPERATE · STARRING · POT OF COFFEE AS DEFENSE · TWINS WITHOUT TALENT · DEAD INXS MEMBER · BLAND WELCOME & OBVIOUS MISTRUST · A THANKLESS HANDJOB · DARBY CRASH'S SWEATY COFFIN · PRODUCED BY · A HORROR CALLED PUBLIC · MAIMED PRIDE & CHALLENGED SELF-ESTEEM · THE BROWN BUBBLY · MUSIC BY · PROSTITUTES OF THE DEAD & AMATEUR SADO EROTIC DRAWINGS · ALCOHOLIC BONFIRE OF IDEAS · THE APOCALYPSE IS A JOKE · STORY BY · LOS ANGELES STILL BIRTH AND THE LEISURE CLASS · DIRECTED BY · WRISTS SLIT WITH BROKEN GLASS IN AN EMPTY BATHTUB IN A FOREIGN COUNTRY

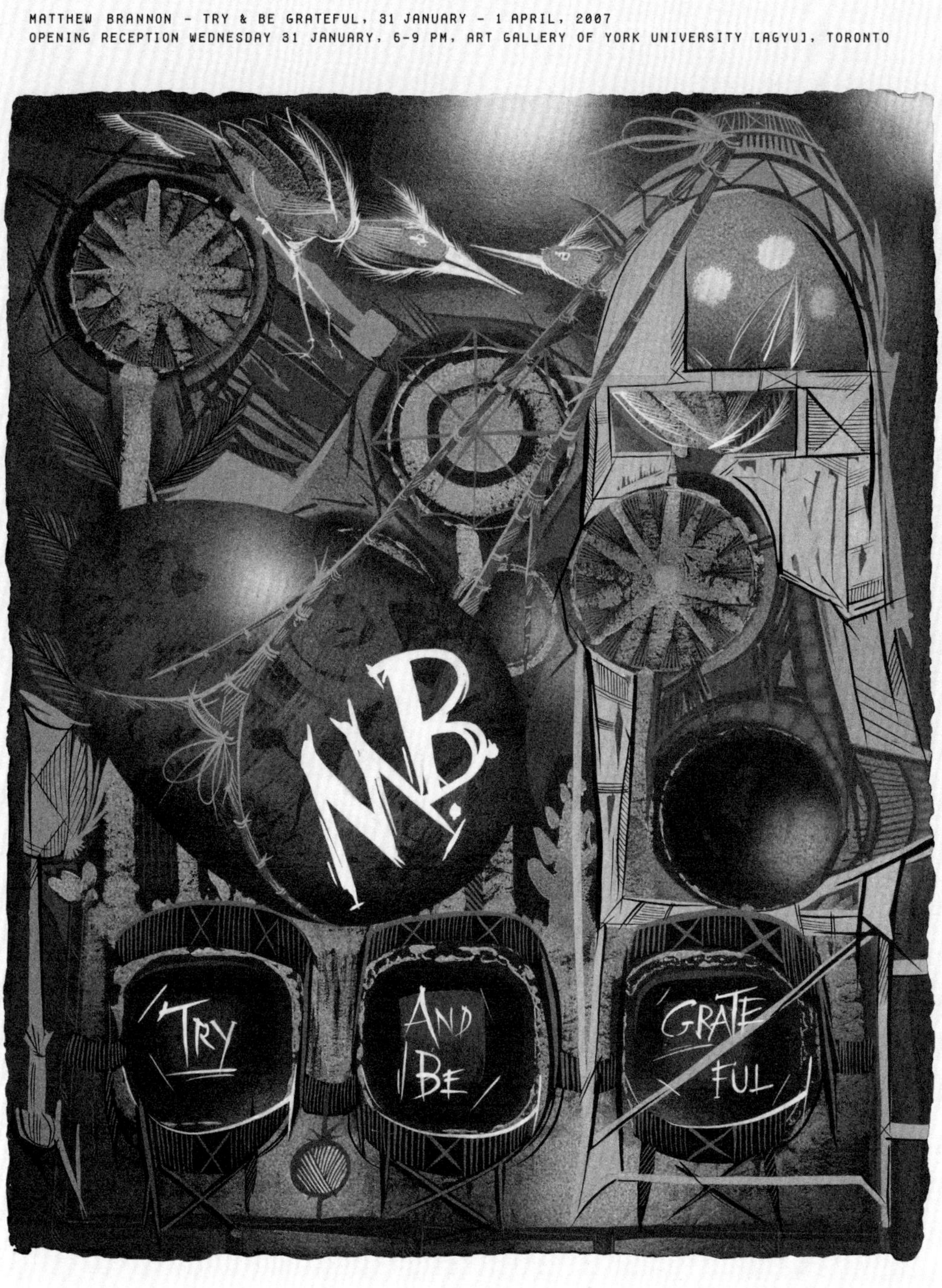

Poster by Lari Pittman, *Matthew Brannon, Try & Be Grateful*, 2007
Offset on paper, 4-color, 27 × 36.5 in. (68.5 × 93 cm)

PAGE 21
Satan's Bedroom, 2001
silkscreen on paper
30 × 22 in. (76.2 × 55.9 cm)
edition of 12
A PESSIMISTIC PRODUCTION · A TWENTIETH CENTURY FOX RELEASE · "SATAN'S BEDROOM" · STARRING · BONELESS BEEF · CORK · UNSALTED SEAHORSE · BONELESS PORK · VODKA · OCELOT PAWS · CO-STARRING · STUFFED PORCUPINE · BOILED PEACOCK · HORSERADISH · CREAMED PEAS · MUSIC BY · SQUID INK SACS · SCREENPLAY BY · POACHED OYSTERS · ORIGINAL STORY BY · MINCED COCKATOO · PRODUCED BY BLOOD OF A PIG & VODKA · DIRECTED BY · BONELESS FISH

PAGE 22
All You Need Is Love, 2006
letterpress on paper
38 × 29 in. (96.5 × 73.7 cm)
edition of 1

PAGE 23
To Choose Wrongly A Career, 2006
letterpress on paper
38 × 29 in. (96.5 × 73.7 cm)
edition of 1

PAGE 25
Vultures & Collectors, 2006
letterpress on paper
24 × 18 in. (61 × 45.7 cm)
edition of 1
PRESSED AGAINST THE WINDOW · PUSHED AGAINST THE TILE · PINNED TO THE FLOOR · BODY FOUND IN THE AFTERNOON · BRIGHT LIGHT ON AN UNMADE BED · CAT RESTS ON BACK · NEVER LIKED TO DANCE · DROVE INTO A PERSONAL WALL · NEVER LIKED JAZZ

PAGE 26
How It All Ends, 2006
letterpress on paper
24 × 18 in. (61 × 45.7 cm)
edition of 1
TUGGING AT YOUR BELT · BRACING YOURSELF FOR THE COLD · SENDING THE KIDS TO REHAB · FEAR STEERS THE METHOD · UNDERSTANDING REVENGE · EXPENSIVE SEXUAL RELATION · INEXPENSIVE SEXUAL RELATION · TOLD HIM WHERE TO PUT IT · LOST THE POINT · THE FORCE OF SAYING NO · THE FORCE OF REGRET

PAGE 27
A Lot Like Trash, 2006
letterpress on paper
24 × 18 in. (61 × 45.7 cm)
edition of 1
AVOIDING FAME · DODGING ACCOUNTABILITY · CROWD PLEASING TEST DRIVE · PRETENDING TO CARE · A CONSERVATIVE VERSION OF RADICAL · A RADICAL VERSION OF CONSERVATIVE · WATCHING IT ALL HAPPEN · ANTICIPATING THE BACKLASH · EVEN PARANOID PEOPLE HAVE ENEMIES

PAGE 29
Less than Sympathetic, 2006
letterpress on paper
24 × 18 in. (61 × 45.7 cm)
edition of 1
DISAPPOINTMENT IS SPECIFIC · ITS TARGET PERSONAL · A PLAGUE OF PERSECUTION FANTASIES ·YOUR SUSPICION PALES · YOUR WORST FEAR REALIZED · THE MISFORTUNES OF VIRTUE · DECISION TO STOP · NOT A POET · PUSHED IN FRONT OF TRAFFIC · CREATING A FEELING OF VACANCY IN OTHERS

PAGE 31
The Price of Admission, 2006
letterpress on paper
24 × 18 in. (61 × 45.7 cm)
edition of 1
THIS IS HOW IT ENDS · THAT WAS HOW IT ENDED · THE APOCALYPSE IS A JOKE · THE LIFE SPAN OF THE WORLD DOES NOT MIRROR HUMAN LIFE · ROCKS IN · SEAS OF DEAD FISH · ANIMALS IN ZOOS DIE DIFFERENTLY THAN IN THE WILD · NEVER THOUGHT YOU HAD IT IN YOU

PAGE 32–33
Try & Be Grateful, 2007
(installation view: *Stage*, 2007)
Art Gallery of York University

PAGE 35
Distraction Becomes You, 2004
letterpress on paper
24 × 18 in. (61 × 45.7 cm)
edition of 3
CHAMPAGNE HEADACHE · WEB LIKE DISTRUST · UNABLE TO FEEL OR CARE OR MAKE DECISIONS

PAGE 37
Loss of Words, 2004
letterpress on paper
24 × 18 in. (61 × 45. 7 cm)
edition of 3
VIN FIN DE TABLE TERRIBLE · WEAK CHOICE · NEVER GO BACK THERE EVER AGAIN PROMISE ME

PAGE 38
Submission, 2004
letterpress on paper
24 × 18 in. (61 × 45.7 cm)
edition of 3
BLANC DE BLANC UNPARDONABLE · 9 GLASSES LATER · EVERYTHING YOU SAY WILL COME BACK TO HURT YOU

PAGE 39
Drunk Baptism, 2004
letterpress on paper
24 × 18 in. (61 × 45.7 cm)
edition of 3
VIN FIN DE TABLE DE GOD · THE FEAR WHICH ORGANIZES YOUR GUILT · EVERYTHING I WANT, YOU HAVE

PAGE 41
End Of The Family Line, 2004
letterpress on paper
24 × 18 in. (61 × 45. 7 cm)
edition of 3
DELUSIONAL SELF-IMPORTANCE BUILDS

PAGE 42
Country Club Upset, 2004
letterpress on paper
24 × 18 in. (61 × 45.7 cm)
edition of 3
SOME THINGS ARE MORE IMPORTANT THAN FAMILY

PAGE 43
Limp Consideration, 2004
letterpress on paper
24 × 18 in. (61 × 45.7 cm)
edition of 3
CAREER TRAIN WRECK ALCHOHOLIC WORKAHOLIC SEEKS SAME

PAGE 45
Disappointed Critic, 2004
letterpress on paper
24 × 18 in. (61 × 45.7 cm)
edition of 3
DIET PILL PARANOIA & PLASTIC TROPHIES

PAGE 47
Hair Of The Dog, 2006
silkscreen on paper
30 × 23 in. (76.2 × 58.4 cm)
edition of 1

PAGE 48
The Last Thing You Remember (His), 2005
letterpress on paper
24 × 17.5 in. (61 × 44.5 cm)
edition of 1
WALL TO WALL MIRRORS IN A PRIVATE BATHROOM AT A PARTY YOU NEED TO LEAVE · PALM TREES BRUSH THE WINDOW · OUTSIDE THE SOUND OF INSECTS · THE CREDIT CARD DOESN'T HAVE YOUR NAME ON IT · SLIDE THE MIRROR RIGHT · SCAN THE PRESCRIPTIONS · SLIDE THE MIRROR LEFT · NOTE THE MOUTHWASH & BAND AIDS · AN ASHED CIGARETTE INSIDE A FORTY FIVE DOLLAR SCENTED CANDLE · BLACK SOAP IN THE SHAPE OF A DOG · PERFUME & POWDER BOTTLES · LOOK AT YOUR GRAY FACE · RUN YOUR HANDS UNDER COLD WATER · RUN YOUR TOUNGE OVER YOUR TEETH · TASTE BLOOD · BREATHE IN AND FLINCH · YOUR COCK NOW HALF ITS SIZE · SWALLOW BITTER PLEGHM · FIGHT THE PANIC · FIGHT THE NAUSEA · THIS ISN'T PART OF YOUR JOB DESCRIPTION · THIS ISN'T THE WAY IT ENDS · THIS IS THE AWFUL LAST OF IT · HOLD THE SINK ON YOUR WAY TO THE FLOOR · LAY YOUR HEAD IN THE PISS SOAKED RUG · TRY TO FOCUS · WAVES OF HEAT & PRESSURE · SOMEONE IS KNOCKING · EVERYONE IS LAUGHING · WISH THAT CANDLE WAS OUT

PAGE 49
The Last Thing You Remember (Hers), 2005
letterpress on paper
24 × 17.5 in. (61 × 44.5 cm)
edition of 1
ONE SEVENTEEN A.M. YOU EXCUSE YOURSELF FROM THE TABLE AT A RESTAURANT YOU CAN NOT AFFORD · SAFE IN THE STALL · YOU REACH BACK AND FLIP THE LATCH · ALREADY ANXIOUS ABOUT LEAVING · YOUR EXPOSED BACK STICKS AGAINST THE GRAY METAL DIVIDER · YOUR HEELS REST ON NOTHING SOLID · YOUR NEW SHOES ARE NO CONSOLATION · THE DAY'S MANICURE REFLECTS YOUR BLACK HOLE EYES ON YOUR BLUE NECK · BREATHE IN · YOU CAN'T FEEL ANY AIR · BREATHE IN · IS YOUR HEART EVEN WORKING · YOUR PULSE ERRATIC AND FAST · WHEN THEY SAID "THAT JOKE ISN'T FUNNY ANYMORE," WERE THEY REFERRING TO YOU · YOU SHOULD DRINK MORE WATER · NEVER LEARN · NEVER AGAIN · YOU SHOULD HAVE STAYED HOME · TRY TO SIT BUT THERE IS NO BENEFIT · YOUR HANDS TOUCH THE COLD WET PORCELAIN · DROP YOUR NECK FORWARD · FEEL YOUR HEART SKIP · YOUR HAIR MAKES A CANOPY

PAGE 50–51
Try & Be Grateful, 2007
(installation view)
Art Gallery of York University

PAGE 52–53
Try & Be Grateful, 2007
(installation view)
Art Gallery of York University

PAGE 55
Fatal Career Misstep, 2005
letterpress on paper
24 × 18 in. (61 × 45.7 cm)
edition of 1
DERIVATIVE & MAGNETIC PAINTING · YOUR SEXUAL HISTORY · OTHER PEOPLES' MONEY · SHELVED FILM · HEROIN TASTE TEST · TEMPERED DISCIPLINE · ONE WEEKS PAY IN ONE NIGHT · TOTALLY GREAT & TOTALLY TRUE · FLOOD OF REGRET · FURIOUS FOSTER PARENT · HORSING AROUND IN BED · YOUNG PLUMBING

PAGE 56
Premature Ejaculation, 2005
letterpress on paper
24 × 18 in. (61 × 45.7 cm)
edition of 1
SUPERFICIAL BURNS SURFACE · POLICE OFFICER GIVING UP · EUROPEAN FURNITURE SHOWROOM · PATIENT HAND JOB · ROLE PLAYING HYENA · PATTERNS OF ABUSE · PALTRY TEMPTATION & AMBIVALENT MAKE OUT · SUCCESSFUL EVENT WITH VODKA · STANDARD TREATMENT · WEAKENED RESOLVE · TOKEN ADDICT · FLUSHED SCREENPLAY · VAGUE TUTOR

PAGE 57
Belligerent Euphoria, 2005
letterpress on paper
24 × 18 in. (61 × 45.7 cm)
edition of 1
THE PASSIVE ART OF COMPLAINING · THE TIME BETWEEN SEIZURES · A PSYCHOLOGICAL BEACHHEAD · STEAMING WET PANT MEAT · APOLOGETIC FANS, FANATICS & FREAKS · SEVERED HANDS OF THE HUNTED · CANNIBAL DELICACIES · LIMP ATTEMPT · HAWKISH HOSTILE PUPPET · DETACHED PARENTS & DIPSOMANIACAL PIONEERS · VULNERABLE SOLDIER

PAGE 58
A Very Upsetting First Novel, 2006
letterpress on paper
34 × 26 in. (86.4 × 66 cm)
edition of 1

PAGE 59
Pushing the Blade in Deeper, 2006
letterpress on paper
34 × 26 in. (86.4 × 66 cm)
edition of 1

PAGE 61
Compliance & Resentment, 2006
silkscreen on paper
24 × 18 in. (61 × 45.7 cm)
edition of 200

PAGE 63
Performance Anxiety, 2006
silkscreen on paper
24 × 18 in. (61 × 45.7 cm)
edition of 200

PAGE 64
Holes in the Armor, 2006
letterpress on paper
38 × 29 in. (96.5 × 73.7 cm)
edition of 1
NIGHTSTAND OF SILVER PICTURE FRAMES & MEDICATION · IMPORTED OXYGEN & ANTIQUE ASHTRAYS · VEINS OVER BONES, UNDER LOOSE SKIN · A GLASS PARROT, A CRYSTAL PAPERWEIGHT, A DECORATIVE INKWELL · MORE GHOST STORY THAN NOVEL · A GRAMMAR TO REVEAL & A GRAMMAR TO DISGUISE CLASS · WE DIE BEFORE READING EVERYTHING WE THOUGHT WE WOULD

PAGE 65
Slut Best Friend, 2006
letterpress on paper
38 × 29 in. (96.5 × 73.7 cm)
edition of 1
SPRAY IT WITH INSECTICIDE · CARPET IT WALL TO WALL · CUT IT IN HALF & HALF AGAIN · CALL IT A PLAN · GO TO RESTAURANTS FEW CAN AFFORD · COLLECT ART · BREED MINIATURE DOGS · BUY CLOTHES FEW COULD WEAR · ATTEMPT HARDCORE · BEG FOR ANOTHER CHANCE · ONCE EXOTIC NOW TEDIOUS · ALWAYS THE ALCOHOLIC · EVEN IN SOBRIETY · EVEN ON DAYS OFF · ESPECIALLY TONIGHT

PAGE 67
Star Becomes Co-Star, 2006
letterpress on paper
38 × 29 in. (96.5 × 73.7 cm)
edition of 1
A NURTURED ADDICTION · DISPOSABLE HEALTH · THE SETTING OF PERSONAL GOALS · THE BENDING OF WILL · THE FEEDING OF FEAR · JEWELRY MADE FROM ENDANGERED ANIMALS · GREAT HEAPS OF FLESH FROM THE SEA · WARM MEAT COVERED IN FLIES · THROATS FILLED WITH CONCRETE · THIS TRUTH HAS NO VALUE · THAT CRITICISM IS SELF SERVING · WOULDN'T YOU WERE A TEACHER · THOUGHT YOU WERE A PARENT

PAGE 68
Los Angeles, 2006
letterpress on paper
38 × 29 in. (96.5 × 73.7 cm)
edition of 1
WHEN THEY HIRED YOU THEY ASKED IF YOU WERE COMFORTABLE WITH IT · ASKED IF YOU'D DONE THIS BEFORE · ESTIMATE THE RISK, ACCEPT THE TERMS · AFRAID TO EVEN ANSWER THE PHONE · HIDE IN THE BATHROOM · PRETEND IT'S FUNNY - YOU MOVING HERE · BLAME YOURSELF · THREATEN OTHERS · TAKE UP SMOKING · STAY HOME TONIGHT

PAGE 69
Crossing Swords, 2006
letterpress on paper
38 × 29 in. (96.5 × 73.7 cm)
edition of 1
I'M DRUNK · I'M WRITING THIS DRUNK · I CAN'T BEAR THE GUILT AND SHAME FOR WHAT I DID · IT MIGHT NOT SEEM LIKE MUCH AFTER YOU READ THIS STORY · BUT IF YOU REALLY FOCUS ON WHAT IT MEANS TO DESTROY TWO COUPLES' LIVES YOU CAN BEGIN TO APPRECIATE HOW SAD IT ALL IS · I'M SURE I'LL GET OVER IT · AND I'M SURE I'LL HAVE SEX AGAIN · BUT I HONESTLY FEEL LIKE I'VE RUINED SO MUCH RIGHT NOW · I'M TOTALLY DRUNK

PAGE 73
Where Were We, 2007
(installation view: *Price Of Admission*, 2007, vinyl on glass)
Whitney Museum of American Art

PAGE 74–75
Where Were We, 2007
(installation view)
Whitney Museum of American Art

PAGE 76
Adult Education, 2007
letterpress on paper
24 × 18 in. (61 × 45.7)
edition of 1
IT'S ABSTRACT · IT'S TOTALLY ABSTRACT · I COPIED IT · I STOLE IT FROM YOU · I RIPPED THE PAGE RIGHT OUT OF THE BOOK · WORD FOR WORD · YOU WEREN'T DOING MUCH WITH IT ANYWAY · UH... · WHEN WE PULL OFF WE MAKE A RIGHT · THEN IT'S ABOUT FIVE MILES BEFORE WE TURN LEFT ONTO THE DIRT ROAD · YOU SHOULD SEE IT ON THE RIGHT · THE PLACE WHERE THE BODIES WERE FOUND

PAGE 77
Pigs Like Us, 2007
letterpress on paper
24 × 18 in. (61 × 45.7 cm)
edition of 1
THEY HAD TO PUMP HER STOMACH · AMAZING WHAT THEY FOUND · AMONG THE ARUGULA, WATERCRESS, BLUE-FIN TUNA, AGE-DRIED STEAK · THERE IT IS · YOUR HEART · AND LOOK ... A BUNCH OF RAZOR BLADES · LITTLE LIGHT BULBS · COCAINE · LITTLE TRAVEL BOTTLES · ANTI-DEPRESSANTS · YOUR OLD UNTOUCHED JOB APPLICATION

PAGE 79
Pulling Out, 2007
letterpress on paper
24 × 18 in. (61 × 45.7 cm)
edition of 1
A BIT AGGRESSIVE? · WOULDN'T YOU SAY? · DIDN'T SEE THAT COMING · THE WAY HE SEEMED PREPARED TO ARGUE AT EVERY TURN · AND WHERE DID HE EVER GET THAT ABOUT YOU KNOW WHAT · SO ANGRY · SOMEWHAT LOST I FEAR · WORRIES ME THOUGH · IT'S AS IF HE'S DETERMINED TO DRAG US DOWN WITH HIM

PAGE 81
The Men in Your Life, 2007
letterpress on paper
24 × 18 in. (61 × 45.7 cm)
edition of 1
TAKES MORE THAN ONE TO FILL THOSE SHOES · THAT'S A PRETTY BIG RESPONSIBILITY TO CARRY · NOT JUST ANYONE COULD DO THIS JOB · EVERY PHONE CALL RESULTS IN ACTION · THINGS THAT CANNOT EASILY BE UNDONE · THAT NO ONE WILL EVER FORGET YOU OF THAT I AM CERTAIN

PAGE 82
Alarm Clock, 2007
letterpress on paper
24 × 18 in. (61 × 45.7 cm)
edition of 1
WHEN HE WRITES HE SEES HIMSELF AS SOMEONE ELSE · AS SOMEONE WHO WRITES WELL · AND WHEN HE TALKS TO OTHERS ABOUT WHAT IT IS HE DOES · HE PICTURES SOMEONE ELSE · A CONVERSATIONALIST BEYOND COMPARE · AND WHEN HE'S HOME AT NIGHT TRYING TO SLEEP · HE SEES HIMSELF AS A GROSS PIG THAT EVERYONE HATES

PAGE 83
Not Young, 2007
letterpress on paper
24 × 18 in. (61 × 45.7 cm)
edition of 1
STEPPING ON A SNAKE'S HEAD · ITS TAIL WRAPPING AROUND YOUR LEG · SPITTING INTO A CAGE · SETTING FIRE TO A NEST · DRAGGING THE OCEAN FLOORS · SERVING THE LAST OF THE MEAT · CLEARING TABLES AND STORING FEARS · WATCHED IT HAPPEN · SAW THE SEX IN FRONT OF EVERYTHING

PAGE 85
Steak Dinner, 2007
letterpress on paper
24 × 18 in. (61 × 45.7 cm)
edition of 1
THIS YEAR TELL HER YOU LOVE HER ALL OVER AGAIN · WITH A GRAB BAG OF DIAMONDS · WITH MOUTHFULS OF CAVIAR · WITH YOUR RENT IN CLOTHES · A CREDIT CARD OF HOTEL ROOMS · STOCKINGS · CHAMPAGNE · PLANE TICKETS · AND A SOFT SLAP ON HER BARE ASS

PAGE 86
Raw Bar, 2007
letterpress on paper
24 × 18 in. (61 × 45.7 cm)
edition of 1
NO - IT WOULDN'T END SO QUICKLY · IT WAS GOING TO BE A MORE DRAWN OUT AFFAIR · I WAS GOING TO HAVE TO LIVE THOSE YEARS · I WAS GOING TO HAVE TO TAKE CARE OF MYSELF · THE NOVEL STARTS WITH THIS IDEA OF AN END · A FILM BEGINS WITH ANOTHER'S CREDITS · WANTED TO TALK ABOUT AN ABUSIVE LIFESTYLE · WANTED TO ADDRESS HOW IT ALL GOES WRONG

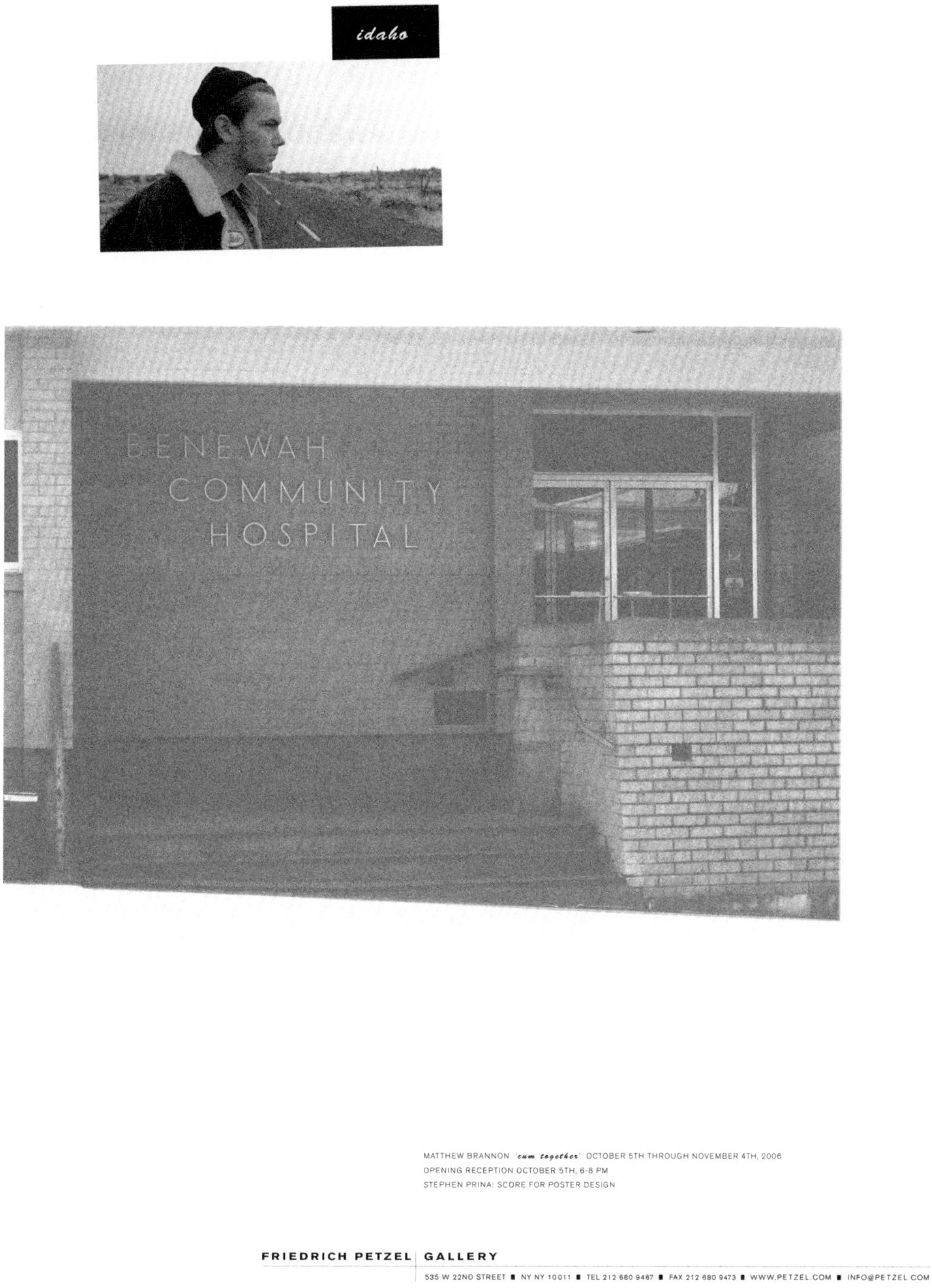

Score for poster design by Stephen Prina, *Matthew Brannon: Cum Together*, 2007
Offset on paper, black and white, 18 × 24 in. (46 × 61 cm)

PAGE 87
Ladies Choice, 2007
letterpress on paper
24 × 18 in. (61 × 45.7 cm)
edition of 1
IT LOOKS RIGHT · BUT IT ISN'T · JUST LOOKS LIKE SOMETHING YOU ALREADY THINK YOU LIKE · BUT MAYBE · JUST MAYBE · YOU DON'T LIKE IT AT ALL · I COULD BE WRONG

PAGE 89
Intellectual Condom, 2007
letterpress on paper
24 × 18 in. (61 × 45.7 cm)
edition of 1
I KNOW YOU KNOW I KNOW · YOU KNOW I KNOW YOU KNOW I KNOW · YOU KNOW I KNOW I KNOW YOU KNOW · I KNOW YOU DIDN'T DO IT · BUT THAT'S NOT WHAT MATTERS NOW

PAGE 91
Say It Again, 2007
letterpress on paper
24 × 18 in. (61 × 45.7 cm)
edition of 1
WHEN YOU READ THIS I WILL BE DEAD · WELL IF NOT REALLY DEAD - THEN ONE DAY · AND YOU TOO - ONE DAY · WILL BE DEAD · BUT EVEN THEN · ONE COULD SAY · THAT YOU HAD READ THIS

PAGE 93
Who Takes Who Home Tonight, 2007
silkscreen on paper
38 × 29 in. (96.5 × 73.7 cm)
edition of 1

PAGE 95
Who Takes Who Home Tonight, 2007
silkscreen on paper
38 × 29 in. (96.5 × 73.7 cm)
edition of 1

PAGE 97
Signature, 2007
letterpress on paper
38 × 29 in. (96.5 × 73.7 cm)
edition of 1
J.F.K. INTERNATIONAL AIRPORT

PAGE 100
Birthday Cake, 2007
letterpress on paper
24 × 18 in. (61 × 45.7 cm)
edition of 1
NOT THE ADVICE I WOULD HAVE GIVEN · BUT - OK, SO SHE KNOWS · IT'S NOT LIKE IT WAS THAT EXPENSIVE · HAS THE TEXTURE OF ... · THE TASTE OF SEAFOOD · REMINDS ME OF SOMETHING I TRIED TO FORGET

PAGE 101
Drinking Games, 2007
letterpress on paper
24 × 18 in. (61 × 45.7 cm)
edition of 1
STEPPING IN SHIT IN PARIS · SLEEPING IN IN TOKYO · BREAKING A FEVER IN BERLIN · CLEANING POOLS IN LOS ANGELES · LOSING HAIR IN LONDON · PAYING FOR IT IN NEW YORK · YOU HAVE TO REPEAT WHAT IT WAS YOU ASKED FOR · SPIT IT OUT BEFORE ANYONE SEES

PAGE 103
Role Models, 2007
letterpress on paper
24 × 18 in. (61 × 45.7 cm)
edition of 1
HAVEN'T READ THIS BEFORE? · I WAS SURE YOU HAD · ENDS BETTER THAN IT BEGINS · AFTER ALL THAT · SHE'S TOO YOUNG · COULDN'T REMEMBER HER LINES · VETERINARIANS · VEGETARIANS · ARCHITECTS AND DOORMEN · A DIPLOMA TO STAND ON · A CAPLESS PEN IN YOUR POCKET

PAGE 105
A Well Pissed On Tree, 2007
letterpress on paper
24 × 18 in. (61 × 45.7 cm)
edition of 1
I DIDN'T SAY THAT · SOMEONE ELSE DID · I'M NOT DRUNK · I MEAN EVEN IF I AM I CAN STILL THINK CLEARLY · PERHAPS CLEARER THAN IF I WAS SOBER · I FEEL LIKE A BAD PERSON ALL THE TIME · SOMETIMES THERE ARE HINTS OF WHAT I'VE DONE RIGHT · BUT REALLY I'M ACTIVELY, CONSTANTLY, AND FURIOUSLY LOOKING FOR SIGNS THAT I'VE DONE SOMETHING WRONG · SHE REMINDS ME CONSTANTLY OF WHAT A LOSER I AM

PAGE 106
But You Do It Anyway, 2007
letterpress on paper
24 × 18 in. (61 × 45.7 cm)
edition of 1
UP TWENTY-FOUR FLOORS · ALL THE WAY IN THE BACK · IN THE SUITE · IN THE BATHROOM · A COUNTER OF COSMETICS · LIPSTICK IN THE SINK · SMASHED GLASS AND TOWELS ON THE FLOOR · PINK LIGHT FROM ABOVE THE MIRRORS · A SHOWER CURTAIN HALF TORN OFF ITS RINGS · WALLPAPER PATTERNED MINT AND BRONZE · THE HUM OF THE AIR CONDITIONING · THE DRIPS IN THE TUB · AN UNANSWERED PHONE RINGING IN THE DARK

PAGE 107
Your Last Name First (for G.C.), 2007
letterpress on paper
24 × 18 in. (61 × 45.7 cm)
edition of 1
AT LAST I UNDERSTOOD WHAT HE WAS TRYING TO SAY · HE WASN'T BEING MEAN AND HE WASN'T ANGRY · HE DIDN'T KNOW A THING · HE HADN'T BEEN BACK TO THE HOTEL · I WAS GOING TO HAVE TO GO TO AFRICA ALONE · I WAS GOING TO HAVE TO BEAR THE HEATED NIGHTS, THE INSECTS, THE CROWDED AIRPORTS · I MIGHT EVEN GET AWAY WITH IT · I WOULD AVOID THE SHAME · BUT I WOULD NEVER SEE YOU AGAIN

PAGE 109
Decide Against, 2007
letterpress on paper
38 × 29 in. (96.5 × 73.7 cm)
edition of 1
WASN'T WHAT WE HOPED FOR · OUR EXPECTATIONS · OUR FEARS · BOTH INAPPROPRIATE AND EXTREME · DIDN'T HIT THE BRAKES FAST ENOUGH · WOKE TO THE SOUND OF GUNS LOADING · TEETH BEING BRUSHED · THE SCRAPE OF THE RAZOR · AGAIN DIET · AGAIN DEBT · AGAIN WAR · AT THE SIDE OF THE STAGE · IN THE DARK · LOOKING OUT · PAST THE GLARING LIGHTS · INTO THE BORED FACES AND PLUSH CHAIRS · IN THE BACK ROW · IN HAND · AN UNLIT CIGARETTE · CLICKING HIS FINGERNAILS WITH THE OTHER · HE CAN READ BETWEEN THE LINES

PAGE 111
Teachers Fuck Students, 2006
silkscreen on paper
24 × 18 in. (61 × 45.7 cm)

PAGE 112
Blow Hard, 2007
letterpress on paper
24 × 18 in. (61 × 45.7 cm)
edition of 1
YES · OH GOD · YES · YES · FUCK YES · THAT'S IT · THAT'S IT · YES · OH GOD · JESUS CHRIST · YES · YES · OH GOD · NO · NO · OH NO · THAT'S IT · YES · YES · FUCK YES

PAGE 113
Blank Check, 2007
letterpress on paper
24 × 18 in. (61 × 45.7 cm)
edition of 1
THAT'S NOT WHAT I'M SAYING · YOU'VE GOT IT ALL WRONG · IT HAS NOTHING TO DO WITH ... I DON'T KNOW THE FIRST THING ABOUT ... I'VE NEVER EVEN BEEN TO ... NOW PULL YOURSELF TOGETHER · YOU KNOW I WOULDN'T ASK IF IT WASN'T IMPORTANT · IT'S NOTHING YOU HAVEN'T DONE BEFORE

PAGE 114
New Money, 2007
letterpress on paper
24 × 18 in. (61 × 45.7 cm)
edition of 1
STOP CRYING · IT ISN'T HELPING · YOU DIDN'T DO THIS · YOU HAVE NOTHING TO DO WITH THIS · YOU SHOULDN'T EVEN BE HERE · JUST WASH YOUR FACE AND GO BACK TO THE HOTEL · AND DON'T SAY ANYTHING · YOU DIDN'T SEE ANYTHING · YOU DIDN'T HEAR ANYTHING · ALL YOU'VE DONE IS WATCH TV AND DRINK

PAGE 115
Hand Lotion, 2007
letterpress on paper
24 × 18 in. (61 × 45.7 cm)
edition of 1
NO, I WISH SHE WAS · MORE OF A SLUT · BUT SHE'S JUST THE NEIGHBOR'S DAUGHTER · THE GIRL GLUED TO THE PHONE · HIGH ON RITALIN AND DIET COKE · ALWAYS TAN AND BARELY DRESSED · JUST THE GIRL YOUR SON GETS TO PLAY STINKY FINGER WITH · NO ONE YOU KNOW

PAGE 117
I'll Be Dining Alone, 2008
silkscreen on paper
44 × 35 in. (111.8 × 89 cm)
edition of 50

PAGE 118
I'm Afraid We're Going To Have To Cancel Our Reservation, 2008
silkscreen on paper
44 × 35 in. (111.8 × 89 cm)
edition of 50

PAGE 119
I Didn't Order This, 2008
silkscreen on paper
44 × 35 in. (111.8 × 89 cm)
edition of 50

PAGE 121
Therapy, 2007
letterpress on paper
24 × 18 in. (61 × 45.7 cm)
edition of 1
People leave therapy because they've hit an issue they're not able to deal with.
People leave therapy because they're unmotivated and not committed.
People leave therapy because they've finished.

PAGE 125
Room Service, 2008
letterpress on paper
22 × 16 in. (55.9 × 40.6 cm)
edition of 1
You catch yourself standing in the check-out line. Embarrassed for yourself. Our definition of art so progressive and yet. Here you are. Buying art supplies at the art supply store. In front of you the undergraduate with a shopping list. Behind you the retired hobbyist. Is this really any job for an adult? Can you really speak of what you do without cringing? A grown man talking about his feelings. When you're introduced to your friends' friends how can you begin to explain what you do?

The fruit goes from rock hard to rotten with no space in between. You hesitate to throw it out. Reminding yourself how much you paid for these exotic vegetables. A fridge full of disintegrating cheese. Of yogurt you consider eating well past its expiration date. A half empty vodka bottle in a narrow frosted cave of an icebox. A couple of frozen chickens you forgot to thaw.

Next to your bed a mountain of half read books. Ambitions abandoned. Introductions read twice. Dog-eared thoughts set aside. After a day spent putting out fires, how could you not drink. Not watch television.

PAGE 127
Rough Trade, 2008
letterpress on paper
22 × 16 in. (55.9 × 40.6 cm)
edition of 1
Guess. No guess again. Think back. No that's not even close. Remember when I told you I did something I shouldn't have done? In New York. That guy in the piano bar? Yeah. Well I did. I fucked him. And he's here tonight. And you were right. He *is* the author.

PAGE 128
Bad Manners, 2008
letterpress on paper
22 × 16 in. (55.9 × 40.6 cm)
edition of 1
Halfway across the intersection you catch yourself mid-thought. The unfinished plate. The second house. A too tight watch. A tap on the shoulder. He wouldn't dare. He hasn't the nerve. This is my sand castle.

PAGE 129
Yes & No, 2008
letterpress on paper
22 × 16 in. (55.9 × 40.6 cm)
edition of 1
His plane lands around seven. When he arrives we've been waiting an hour or more. He's been drinking all day but he pretends it's his first. He tells us how he sat next to this very successful third-rate actor. About dinner the night before in Shanghai with a museum director and how they shared a similar anxiety concerning their future roles.

And now his hand indiscreetly touches yours. Reaching for more salt. Coughing when he asks if you like the wine. After dinner someone suggests charades. You decline and sit at the piano. Adjusting your incidental music to follow the game of frustrated mutes and spastic trivia. A cheap *Lolita*, a blunt *Razor's Edge*.

In bed at night we revisit the day's conversations. Waiting for the light. Hoping the morning isn't a myth.

PAGE 131
Not Necessary, 2008
letterpress on paper
22 × 16 in. (55.9 × 40.6 cm)
edition of 1
Before we begin. I'd like to thank everyone who made this evening possible. First there's ... whose countless hours and faith in this project ... And ... who took the bullet when ... And ... whose selflessness opened many doors once closed. And of course ... who knew what questions to ask and which to avoid, who provided the rent when there was none. And to the late ... you are in all our thoughts tonight.

PAGE 132
An Actor's Actor, 2008
letterpress on paper
22 × 16 in. (55.9 × 40.6 cm)
edition of 1
Finish your drink. We're leaving.

PAGE 133
R.S.V.P., 2008
letterpress on paper
22 × 16 in. (55.9 × 40.6 cm)
edition of 1
Being polite is key to living in a major metropolitan center. Whether it's consideration when hailing a cab, letting people exit before you enter, or not chewing gum in public. It's important. But you might also consider that wearing fur is offensive and obnoxious to most. Or that wearing an expensive suit but not shaving is patronizing. And never start a sentence with...

That's funny I was sure I had locked the front door when we left.

PAGE 135
Sore Throat, 2008
letterpress on paper
22 × 16 in. (55.9 × 40.6 cm)
edition of 1
Kids don't give it away for free. Steer the boat away from the shore. Everything you have counts. Everything they offer costs. Condoms are but... These nights, foggy notions. When they say it doesn't hurt – they lie.

More than you know.

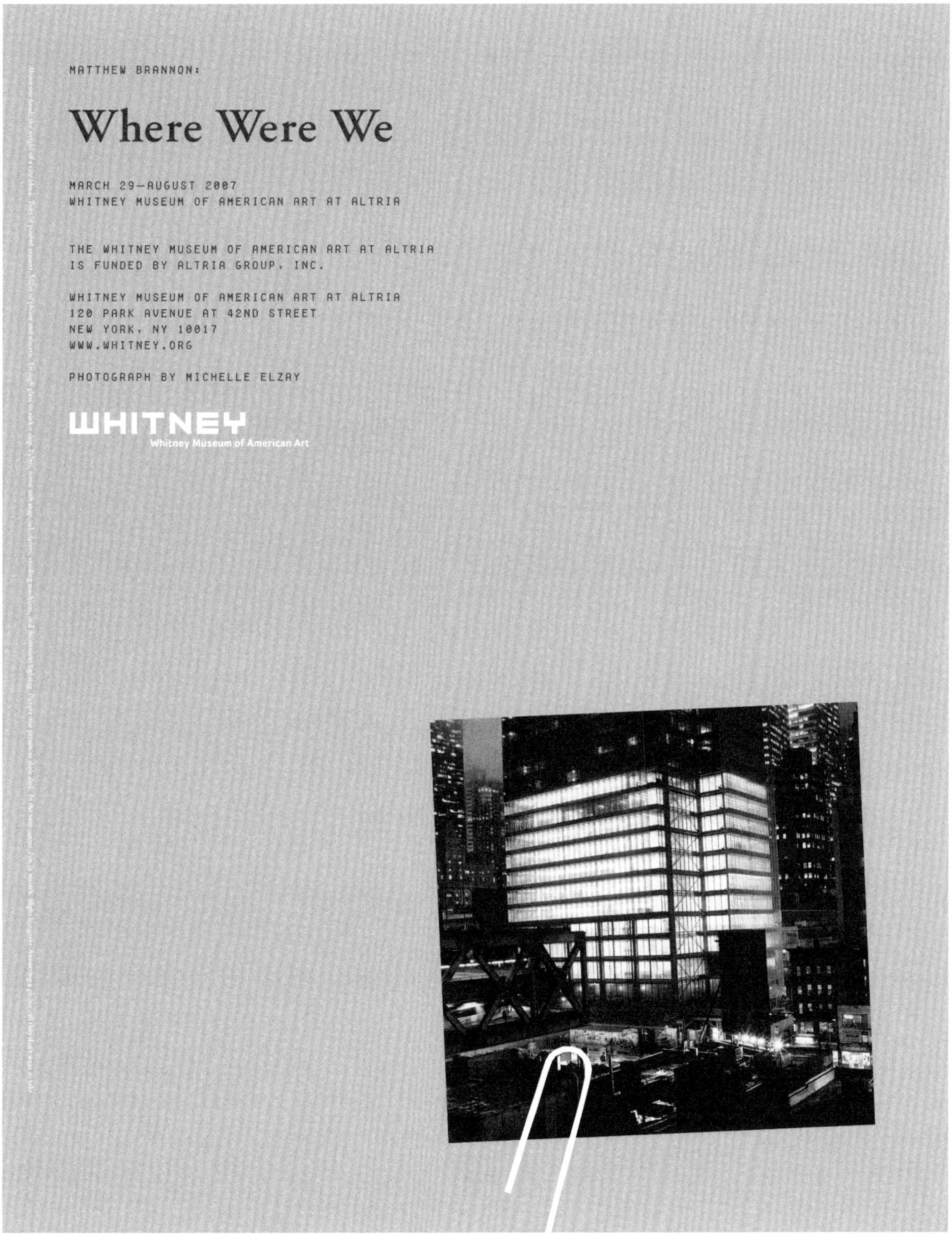

Poster by Michelle Elzay, *Matthew Brannon: Where We Were*, 2007
Offset on paper, 4-color, 18 × 24 in. (46 × 61 cm)

Selected Biography & Bibliography

b. 1971, St. Maries, Idaho
Lives and works in New York

EDUCATION

1999 MFA, Columbia University, New York
1995 BA, University of California, Los Angeles

SOLO EXHIBITIONS

2008 *The Question is a Compliment*, Friedrich Petzel Gallery, New York
Before You Say No, Galleria Gio Marconi, Milan
2007 *Where Were We*, Whitney Museum of American Art at Altria, New York
Try & Be Grateful, AGYU, Art Gallery of York University, Toronto
2006 *Cum Together*, Friedrich Petzel Gallery, New York
Shoegazers & Graverobbers, Art 37 Statements, David Kordansky Gallery, Basel
Hyena, Jan Winkelmann/Berlin, Berlin
2005 *Meat Eating Plants*, David Kordansky Gallery, Los Angeles
Penetration, Jan Winkelmann/Berlin, Berlin
2004 *Exhausted Blood & Imitation Salt*, John Connelly Presents, New York
2003 *Tatum O'Neals Birthday Party*, Kevin Bruk Gallery, Miami
2000 *Soft Rock*, Künstlerhaus Bethanien, Berlin

SELECTED GROUP EXHIBITIONS

2008 Whitney Biennial, Whitney Museum of American Art, New York
One Day I Woke Up Very Early, Office Baroque Gallery, Antwerp
50 Moons of Saturn, T2 Torino Triennale, curated by Daniel Birnbaum, Turin
Galerie Chez Valentine, Paris
2007 *Multiplex: Directions in Art, 1970 to Now*, curated Deborah Wye, Museum of Modern Art New York, New York
On the Marriage Broker Joke, curated by Wim Peeters, Office Baroque Gallery, Antwerp
(the) Melvins @ (the) Mandrake, curated by Bob Nickas, The Mandrake, Los Angeles
Uncertain States of America: American Art in the 3rd Millenium, curated by Daniel Birnbaum, Hans Ulrich Obrist and Gunnar Kvaran, Le Musée du Serignan, Serignan; Herning Art Museum, Copenhagen; The Centre for Contemporary Art, Zanek Ujazdowski, Warsaw
2006 *Bring the War Home,* QED Gallery, Los Angeles
Uncertain States of America: American Art in the 3rd Millenium, The Center for Curatorial Studies, Bard College, Annandale-on-Hudson; Reykjavik Art Museum, Reykjavik; Serpentine Gallery, London

666, curated by Jan Tumlir, USC Roski School of Fine Arts
Social Design, Badischer Kunstverein, Karlsruhe
Exquisite Corpse, Mitchell Algus Gallery, curated by Bob Nickas, New York
Matthew Brannon, Wade Guyton, Patrick Hill, United Artists. Ltd., Marfa
Slow Burn, curated by Jonah Freeman, Galerie Edward Mitterrand, Geneva

2005 *Uncertain States of America: American Art in the 3rd Millenium,* Astrup Fearnley Museum of Modern Art, Oslo
Passion Beyond Reason, Wallstreet 1, Berlin, a Miller/Rockenschaub Project
Temporary Import, Art Forum Berlin, Special Exhibitions, Berlin,
Threshold, Max Wigram, London
New Tapestries, Sara Meltzer, New York
We Could Have Invited Everyone, curated by Peter Coffin, Andrew Kreps Gallery, New York
The Most Splendid Apocalypse, curated by Jason Murison, PPOW, New York
Post No Bills, curated by Matthew Higgs, White Columns, New York
There Is a City in My Mind, Southfirst, New York
Wordplay, Julie Saul Gallery, New York
Lesser New York, A Fia Backström Production, New York
Greater New York, PS1/MoMA, New York
We love Amerika, Jan Winkelmann/Berlin, Berlin
On the Beach, curated by Justin Lowe, Printed Matter, New York

2004 *Halloween Horror Films,* Southfirst, New York
If Direction Is a Look, with Sarah Morris, Galería Javier López, Madrid
Besides, popularity is a rather lumpy concept, no?, curated by Raif Brog and Petra Rinck, Kunsthalle Düsseldorf
Summer Summary, curated by Roger White, temporary space, New York
Noctambule, D'Amelio Terras at The Fondation Dosne: Bibliotheque Thiers, Paris
Curious Crystals of Unusual Purity, curated by Bob Nickas and Steve Lafrenier, PS1/MoMA, New York
Tapestry from an Asteroid, Golinko Kordansky Gallery, Los Angeles
Hohe Berge, Tiefes Tal, Autocenter, Berlin, Curated by Markus Draper
Collection: How I Spent a Year, curated by Bob Nickas, PS1/MoMA, New York
Lumpen Decadents, curated by Gean Moreno, Ingalls & Associates, Miami
Cave Canem, John Connelly Presents, New York

2003 *Kult 48 Klubhouse,* curated by Scott Hug, Deitch Projects, New York
Snowblind, with Wade Guyton & Mungo Thomson, John Connelly Presents, New York
My people were fair and had cum in their hair (but now they're content to spray the stars from your boughs), curated by Bob Nickas, Team Gallery, New York
Inaugural Exhibition, Golinko Kordansky Gallery, Los Angeles
I'm Afraid of Everything, Blonde Revolution, New York
Escape from New York, curated by Jason Murison, Summit Art Center, Summit, New Jersey
Corporate Profits vs. Labor Costs, D'Amelio Terras, New York

Parking Lot, Ten in One Gallery, New York
The Melvins, curated by Bob Nickas, Anton Kern Gallery, New York
Late to Work Everyday, curated by Noah Sheldon, DuPreau Gallery, Chicago
Talking Pieces, Text and Image in Contemporary Art, curated by Ute Riese, Museum Morsbroich, Leverkusen, Germany

2002 *Triple Theatre*, with Heidie Giannotti, Triple Candie, New York
Dark Spring, curated by Nicolaus and Liam Gillick, Ursula Blickle Stiftung, Kraichtal

2001 *Dedalic Convention*, curated by Liam Gillick and Annette Kosak, MAK, Vienna

2000 *Luggage*, curated by Matthew Brannon, Galerie Max Hetzler, Berlin
@, curated by Jason Murison, PPOW Gallery, New York

1999 *Made Especially for You*, curated by Jenelle Porter, Artists Space, New York
The Wight Biennial, curated by Mungo Thomson, The New Wight Gallery, Los Angeles
MFA Thesis Exhibition, curated by Thelma Golden, Columbia University, New York

1998 *1 + 3 = 4 x 1*, collaboration with Liam Gillick, curated by Susanne Gaensheimer Galerie fur Zeitgenossische Kunst Liepzig
Oh My God I live on the thirteenth floor in Holland, which doesn't exist in the United States, or no?, collaboration with George Rush, curated by Jay Batlle, H. Cleyndertweg 13 space, Amsterdam

1996 *Paint as Purpose*, curated by Roger Ray and Jesse H. Rivard, Purple Gallery, Los Angeles
New Memory, curated by Slater Bradley, Spanish Kitchen Studios, Los Angeles

SELECTED BIBLIOGRAPHY

2008 Arlien-Soborg, Mads. "Artist Must-haves," *Dansk* edition 17, 2008, p. 46–47, ill.
Turvey, Lisa. "Matthew Brannon," *Whitney Biennial 2008* exhibition catalogue, Whitney Museum of American Art, 2008, pp. 108–109, ill.

2007 Brannon, Matthew "Use Value," *Heather Rowe: Shards*, catalogue, D'Amelio Terras, p. 54–55, ill.
Bryant, Eric. "Paint It Bleak," *Art News*, December 2007, pp. 128–131, ill.
"Artist Projects: CMYK," *Cabinet*, Issue 27, Fall 2007, pp. 36–37 ill., curated by Walead Beshty.
Wolff, Rachel. "Young Masters," *New York Magazine*, October 15, 2007, p. 48, ill.
Brannon, Matthew, "Out-of-body Experience," *The New York Times Style Magazine*, pp. 276–279, ill.
Brannon, Matthew, "Eel at Ease," *V Magazine*, Fall Preview 2007, p. 69, ill.
Brown, Nicholas. "The Language of Success: Anxiety and excess in Matthew Brannon's *Try & Be Grateful*," *Color Magazine*, vol. 5, no. 2, pp. 98-107 ill.

Kunitz, Daniel. "A Wicked Ventriloquist," *The New York Sun*, June 14, 2007, p. 20, ill.
Schwendener, Martha. "Whitney Museum at Altria: Matthew Brannon, 'Where Were We'," *The New York Times*, May 18, 2007, p. 25.
"Matthew Brannon, 'Where Were We'," *The New Yorker*, May 14, 2007, p. 24.
Ratner, Megan. "Tongue in Chic: The guilty pleasure of looking at Matthew Brannon's slyly subversive posters," *Art on Paper*, May–June 2007, vol. 11, no. 5, pp. 50–55, cover ill. and ill.
Listings Editor. "Matthew Brannon, 'Where Were We'," *Time Out New York*, April 26–May 2, 2007, p. 110, ill.
Listings Editor. "Matthew Brannon," *Monopol*, April 2007, p. 124, ill.
Scott, Andrea K. "Matthew Brannon, 'Where Were We'," *Time Out New York*, April 12–18, 2007, p. 86, ill.
Schwendener, Martha, "Material Muse for Some Strange Bedfellows," *The New York Times*, April 6, 2007, p. E34, ill.
Milroy, Sarah. "A Riot of Dark Fragments," *Toronto Globe and Mail*, March 1, 2007, ill.
Feldman, Jenny. "Beautiful Dreamers," *Elle*, March 2007, p. 198, ill.
2006 Ellis, Patricia. "Matthew Brannon," *USA Today: New American Art from The Saatchi Gallery* exhibition catalogue, Royal Academy of Arts, 2006 pp. 60–69, ill.
Lawrence, Vanessa. "Graphic Art," *Women's Wear Daily*, October 5, 2006, p. 4, ill.
Muhle, Maria. "Mood Swings," *Texte Zur Kunst*, September 2006, pp. 194–96, ill.
Funcke, Bettina A.W., ed. Allen Ruppersberg, Seth Price, Matthew Brannon, Donald Judd, and Johanna Burton, *Continuous Project #8*, Chatou, France: CNEAI, Paris, 2006, pp. 56–57, ill.
Cotter, Holland. "At a Group Show in Chelsea, the Art is Sharp but the Categories Blurry," *The New York Times*, August 16, 2006.
Ward, Ossian. "Matthew Brannon: impenetrable collectible," *The Art Newspaper*, Art Basel Daily Edition, June 14, 2006, p. 8.
Cromwell, Wendy. "Buying into a Trend," *Art on Paper*, May/June 2006, p. 22.
Pavone, Rosa. "Never Innocent, Casual, or Involuntary: An Interview with Matthew Brannon," *Uovo,* April 2006, pp. 138–155, ill.
Blom, Ina. "The Young Americans," *Texte Zur Kunst*, March 2006, pp. 169–173.
Tumlir, Jan. "Openings: Jan Tumlir on Matthew Brannon," *Artforum*, February 2006, pp. 196–197.
North Drive Press, multiple, Issue 3, 2006 New York.
2005 *Uncertain States of America: American Art in the 3rd Millenium* (exh. cat.), Astrup Fearnley Museum of Modern Art, Oslo, 2005, pp. 30–33, ill.
Parkett, insert, Issue 73, New York/Zurich.
SITE, insert, Issue 8, Düsseldorf.
Mixburgh, General Store at SPACE, cassette, Pittsburgh, curated by Tyson Reeder.

2004 White, Roger. "In Conversation: Matthew Brannon with Roger White," *The Brooklyn Rail*, April 2004.

2003 Poster Project in 3 Locations, SITE Ausstellungsraum, Düsseldorf, Art Frankfurt, Frankfurt & Reg Vardy Gallery, London, curated by Ralf Brog & Petra Rinck.

K48, Religion & Cult Issue, *K48 Magazine*, New York.

Charley Magazine, Ed. Maurizio Cattelan, Bettina Funcke, Massimiliano Gioni, Ali Subotnick.

2002 *SITE*, insert, Issue 6, Düsseldorf.

Open City, insert, Issue 16, New York, Ed. Mungo Thomson.

2001 *The UKS Biennial*, book jacket, Norway, Collaboration with Heidie Giannotti.

ARTIST'S WRITINGS

2008 Brannon, Matthew, "Questionnaire," *Frieze*, March 2008, p. 200.

Brannon, Matthew, "Family Guide by Matthew Brannon," Whitney Biennial 2008, 10-page brochure.

2007 Brannon, Matthew, "Who is Guy de Cointet?" *Artforum*, Summer 2007, p. 414.

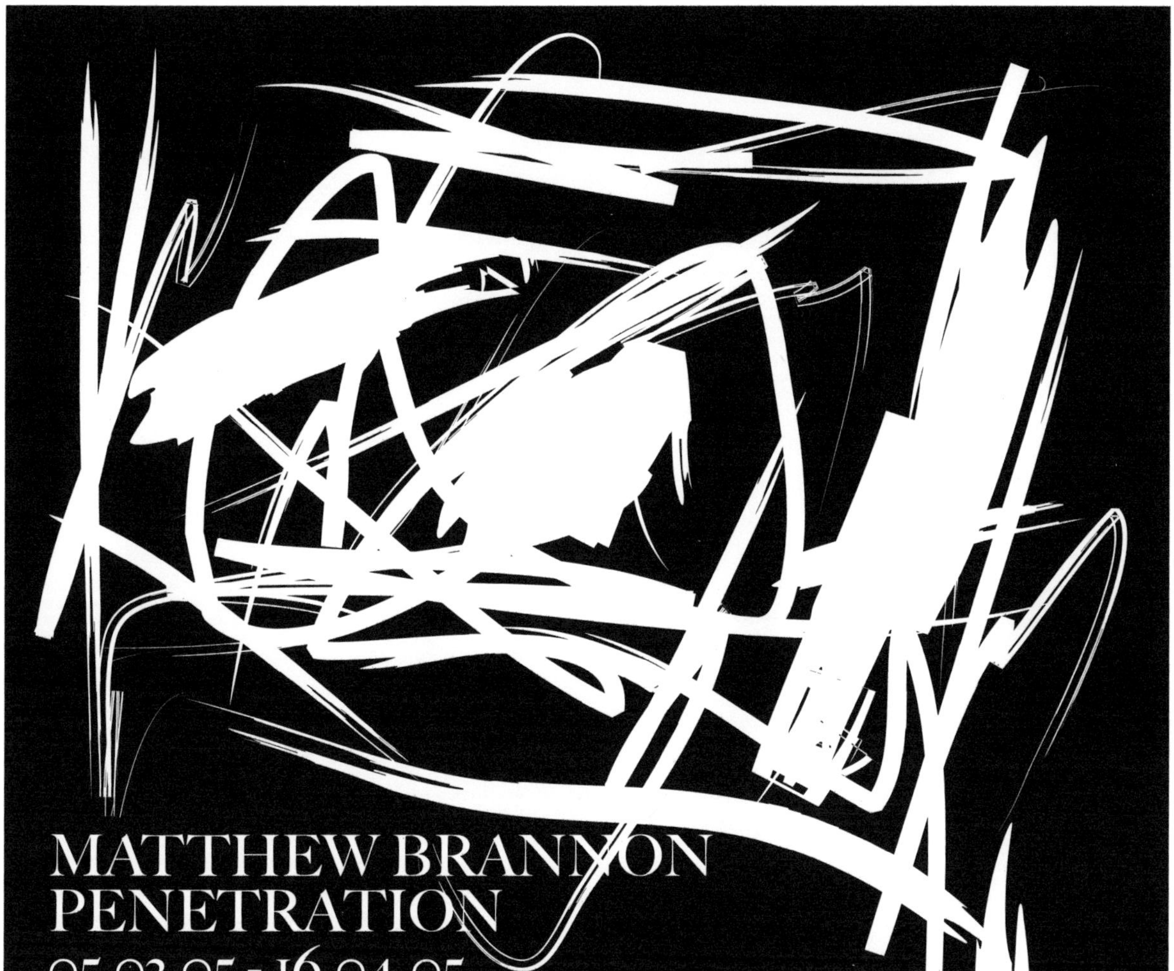

Poster by Liam Gillick, *Matthew Brannon: Penetration*, 2005
Offset on paper, black and white, 24 × 34 in. (60 × 86 cm)

Acknowledgements

An AGYU Founders Presentation, both the exhibition *Try & Be Grateful* and this publication have been supported by Carol and David Appel, Salah J. Bachir, Hal Jackman Foundation, Steven and Lynda Latner, Philip B. Lind, Nancy McCain and Bill Morneau, Julia and Gilles Ouellette, Carol and Morton Rapp, Laura Rapp and Jay Smith, Judy Schulich and David Stein, and Sandra L. Simpson. As well, the Friedrich Petzel Gallery, New York and David Kordansky Gallery, Los Angeles have generously assisted the publication of this book. At the AGYU, Emelie Chhangur has been essential to all aspects of this project having already introduced Brannon to the Gallery through a residency in 2005. Her contribution has been invaluable.

P. M.

For the exhibition *Try & Be Grateful* and the catalogue *To Say the Very Least* I would like to thank the following individuals for their energy, consideration and enthusiasm: Barbara Balfour, Jay Batlle, Carol Bove, Nicholas Brown, Anton Chan, Howie Chen, James Crane, Luther Davis, Nathaniel Davis, Natasha Garcia-Lomas, Shay Gibson, Sydney Gilbert, Liam Gillick, Konstantin Grab, David Kordansky, Eric Matthews, Michael Maranda, Will Munro, Friedrich Petzel, Lari Pittman, Bob Rennie, Maureen Sarro, Jon Sasaki, Noah Sheldon, Mika Tajima, Sam Tsao, Jan Tumlir, and Paul Wagner. And especially Emelie Chhangur and Philip Monk to whom I owe more than I can say. To work with people of such limitless generosity, whether measured in wine, words, or white walls, has spoiled me forever. And to everyone who read a word. That moment we shared. But to none more than Michelle Elzay, Alex Kasavin, and Anthony Mazzella.

M. B.

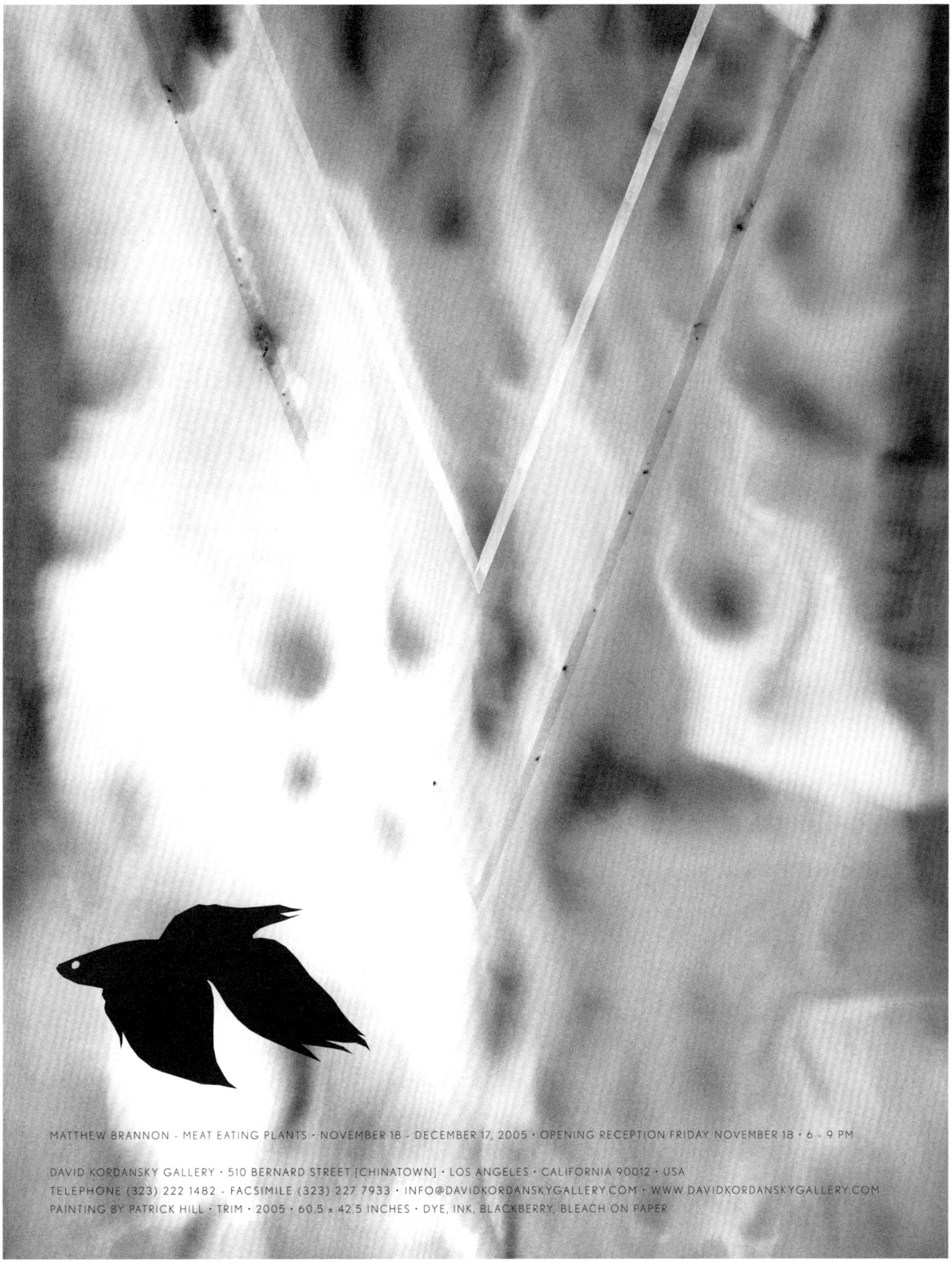

Poster by Patrick Hill, *Matthew Brannon: Meat Eating Plants*, 2005
Offset on paper, 4-color, 18 × 24 in. (46 × 61 cm)

With much thanks to the following individuals and collections:

Collection de Bruin-Heijn
PAGE: 64, 69

Collection of Andy Stillpass, Cincinnati, Ohio
PAGE: 65

Collection of Debi and Steven Wisch
PAGES: 114, 115

Collection of Gio Marconi, Milan
PAGE: 100

Collection of Gregory Papadimitriou, Athens
PAGES: 48, 49

Collection of Jaime Johnson, New York
PAGE: 68

Collection of Kasumi Koji, Tokyo
PAGE: 7

Collection of Maja Hoffmann, Switzerland
PAGE: 59

Collection of Nancy Stillpass, New York
PAGE: 121

Collection of Thea Westreich and Ethan Wagner, New York
PAGES: 3, 26

Collection of Warren and Allison Kanders, Connecticut
PAGES: 76, 77, 79, 81, 82, 83, 85, 86, 87, 89, 91

Collection Passas, Greece
PAGE: 105

Courtesy of the artist and Friedrich Petzel Gallery, New York
PAGES: 73, 101, 107

Courtesy of the artist, Friedrich Petzel Gallery, New York and David Kordansky Gallery, Los Angeles
PAGES: 5, 9, 125, 127, 128, 129, 131, 132, 133, 135

Private Collection
PAGE: 106

Private Collection, Boston
PAGES: 67, 93, 95

Private Collection, Courtesty of BFAS Blondeau Fine Art Services, Geneva
PAGES: 23, 27, 58, 97, 112, 113

Private Collection, London
PAGE: 31

Raiola Collection, Rome
PAGE: 103

Rennie Collection, Vancouver
PAGES: 55, 56, 57

Ringier Collection, Switzerland
PAGE: 29

Rubell Family Collection, Miami
PAGES: 22, 25

The Museum of Modern Art, New York
PAGE: 109

The Saatchi Gallery, London
PAGE: 47

Photo Credits:

Cheryl O'Brien
(AGYU installation photographs)
PAGES: 12–13, 32–33, 50–51, 52–53

Jason Mandella
PAGES: 112, 113, 114, 115

Lamay Photo
PAGES: 5, 7, 15, 17, 18, 19, 45, 58, 59, 64, 65, 67, 68, 69, 73, 74–75, 76, 77, 79, 81, 82, 83, 85, 86, 87, 89, 91, 93, 95, 97, 100, 101, 103, 121

Noah Sheldon
PAGES: 3, 21, 22, 23, 25, 26, 27, 29, 31, 35, 37, 38, 39, 47, 55, 56, 57, 61, 63, 109, 111

Robert Wedemeyer
PAGES: 117, 118, 119

Thomas Mueller
PAGES: 9, 41, 42, 43, 48, 49, 105, 106, 107, 125, 127, 128, 129, 131, 132, 133, 135